William Pitt
The Younger
1759–1806
A Bibliography

Meckler's Bibliographies of British Statesmen

Series Editor: Gregory Palmer

1. William Pitt the Younger 1759–1806: A Bibliography
   A. D. Harvey
   ISBN 0-88736-314-8 CIP 1989

2. Lord Grenville 1759–1834: A Bibliography
   A. D. Harvey
   ISBN 0-88736-313-X CIP 1989

3. George Grenville: A Bibliography
   Rory T. Cornish
   ISBN 0-88736-306-7 CIP *forthcoming*

4. Charles James Fox: A Bibliography
   David Schweitzer
   ISBN 0-88736-296-6 CIP *forthcoming*

5. Lord Curzon: A Bibliography
   James G. Parker
   ISBN 0-88736-308-8 CIP *forthcoming*

6. Neville Chamberlain: A Bibliography
   Stephen Stacey
   ISBN 0-88736-294-X CIP *forthcoming*

7. Lord Nelson: A Bibliography
   Leonard Cowie
   ISBN 0-88736-295-8 CIP *forthcoming*

8. Robert Harley: A Bibliography
   Alan Downie
   ISBN 0-88736-286-9 CIP *forthcoming*

9. William Ewart Gladstone: A Bibliography
   Nicholas Adams
   ISBN 0-88736-361-X CIP *forthcoming*

10. The Duke of Wellington: A Bibliography
    Michael Partridge
    ISBN 0-88736-297-4 CIP *forthcoming*

11. Lord North: A Bibliography
    Rory T. Cornish
    ISBN 0-88736-292-3 CIP *forthcoming*

12. Sir Robert Walpole: A Bibliography
    Alan Downie
    ISBN 0-88736-284-2 CIP *forthcoming*

WILLIAM PITT THE YOUNGER 1759–1806
A Bibliography

A. D. Harvey

Bibliographies of
British Statesmen
no. 1

Meckler
Westport • London

Library of Congress Cataloging-in-Publication Data

Harvey, A. D. (Arnold D.)
    William Pitt the younger, 1759–1806 : a bibliography / A.D. Harvey.
      p. cm.—(Meckler's bibliographies of British statesmen : 1)
    Bibliography: p.
    Includes index.
    ISBN 0-88736-314-8 (alk. paper) : $
      1. Pitt, William, 1759–1806—Bibliography. 2. Great Britain—Politics and government—1760–1820—Bibliography. I. Title.
II. Series.
Z8694.H37   1989
[DA522.P6]
016.94107′3′0924—dc19   89-2791
                                                                                                             CIP

British Library Cataloguing in Publication Data

Harvey, A.D.
    William Pitt the younger 1759–1806:
    a bibliography.—(Bibliographies of
    British statesmen)
    1. Great Britain. Pitt, William, 1759–1806
    —Bibliographies
    I. Title II. Series
    016.94107′3′0924

ISBN 0-88736-314-8

Copyright © 1989 Meckler Corporation. All rights reserved. No part of this publication may be reproduced in any form by any means without prior written permission from the publisher, except by a reviewer who may quote brief passages in review.

Meckler Corporation, 11 Ferry Lane West, Westport, CT 06880.
Meckler Ltd., Grosvenor Gardens House, Grosvenor Gardens,
   London SW1W 0BS, U.K.

Printed on acid free paper.
Printed and bound in the United States of America.

Contents

INTRODUCTION	1
CHRONOLOGY OF SIGNIFICANT EVENTS IN THE LIFE OF WILLIAM PITT	9
I. UNPUBLISHED PERSONAL PAPERS	
A. Great Britain	13
B. United States of America	22
II. PUBLISHED COMPILATIONS OF ORIGINAL PAPERS	
A. Historical Manuscripts Commission Reports	25
B. Other Collections	26
III. OTHER WORKS PRINTING LETTERS FROM PITT *IN EXTENSO*	29
IV. SPEECHES	31
V. PUBLISHED WRITINGS OF PITT	33
VI. PAMPHLETS ETC. RELATING TO PITT	
A. Satirical Attacks on Pitt	35
B. Other Pamphlets Dealing with Pitt:	40
Constitutional Crisis of 1783–1784	40
Parliamentary Reform	40
The War with France	40
Public Finance	41
The State of the Poor	43
The Legislative Union with Ireland	43
Pitt's First Administration Generally	43
Pitt's Relations with the Addington Ministry	44
Pitt's Second Administration	46

Tributes and Criticisms of Pitt after his Death	46
Poetic Tributes to Pitt	47
VII. NEWSPAPERS	49
VIII. BIOGRAPHIES OF PITT	53
IX. CONTEMPORARY MEMOIRS AND DIARIES ETC. CONTAINING IMPORTANT MATERIAL ON PITT	59
X. SPECIAL TOPICS:	63
Pitt's Relations with the Earl of Shelburne 1782–1783	63
Pitt's Establishment in Power, and Style of Government	63
Pitt's Peacetime Financial Administration	65
Pitt and the French Revolution	66
Accession of the Portland Whigs to Pitt's Government	67
Conduct of the War with France	67
The Legislative Union with Ireland	68
The Campaign to Abolish the Slave Trade	69
Relations with Henry Addington after 1801	69
XI. PORTRAITS ETC.	71
XII. PLACES ASSOCIATED WITH PITT	73
INDEX OF AUTHORS AND TITLES	75
INDEX OF CORRESPONDENTS AND TOPICS	79

Mr Pitt had foibles, and of course, they were not diminished by so long a continuance in office; but for a clear and comprehensive view of the most complicated subject in all its relations; for that fairness of mind which disposes a man to follow out, and when overtaken to recognise the truth; for magnanimity, which made him ready to change his measures, when he thought the good of the country required it, though he knew he should be charged with inconsistency on account of the change; for willingness to give a fair hearing to all that could be urged against his own opinions, and to listen to the suggestions of men, whose understanding he knew to be inferior to his own; for personal purity, disinterestedness, integrity, and love of his country, I have never known his equal.

William Wilberforce to W. Hey, 12 February 1806. Robert Isaac and Samuel Wilberforce. *The Life of William Wilberforce,* 5 vols. (London, 1838), 3: 249–250.

William Pitt, in an engraving by A. Cardon, from a bust by I. Flaxman.

Introduction

WILLIAM PITT was prime minister for nearly nineteen crucial years, a record exceeded only by Sir Robert Walpole; yet when he died he was only 46, the age at which Walpole *began* his long ministry. Easily the youngest man ever to be prime minister of Britain, he also held the record as youngest cabinet minister, having been appointed Chancellor of the Exchequer in the Earl of Shelburne's administration on 6 July 1782, a few weeks after his 23rd birthday. His career was thus remarkable, yet his achievement seems ambiguous. He appeared to have been a major success as a reforming peacetime minister between 1784 and 1793 but a failure subsequently as war leader in the great struggle with Revolutionary France (though those who followed after him were for a long time no more successful). He was responsible for the establishment of the Sinking Fund (1786), the policy of opposing Russian expansionism in south-eastern Europe (1791), the first British Income Tax (1798), and the Union with Ireland (1800), but the merit of all these measures (or at least Pitt's version of them) has come to be questioned. In his lifetime he dominated not only the political scene of his own country but also the councils of Europe, for it was he who was recognised from 1793 onwards as the leader of the continent's resistance to the ambitions of Revolutionary France; but subsequently, after the applause had died away and his memory had begun to fade, he appeared more and more a master of sterile expedients, a hollow imitation of a leader, a fake giant surrounded by real pygmies, and deriving his greatness only from the littleness of his admirers.

He was the son of William Pitt, later 1st Earl of Chatham, Britain's great war leader during the Seven Years' War, and of Hester, daughter of Richard Grenville of Wotton Hall, Buckinghamshire. George Grenville, prime minister 1763–1765 and notorious as author of the Stamp Act, was his uncle. He inherited something of the appearance—tall, thin, stiff and imperious—of his father, but not his passionate, hypochondriacal, almost unbalanced nature. The enormous reputation of his father undoubtedly assisted the extraordinarily speedy recognition of his precocious talents, but it is possible he inherited as much from his mother's side of the family. A peculiarity of his Grenville cousins, shared by both Pitt and his older brother John, 2nd Earl of Chatham, was their apparent deficiency in procreative instinct. They belonged to a culture which still showed a frank interest in sexual intercourse, and some of Pitt's Grenville cousins, as well as his brother, had hereditary peerages which they would normally have wished to pass on to their sons. But of the seven male grandchildren of Richard Grenville, four did not marry, and only one managed to have children. As a young man astonishingly promoted to the head of government, Pitt's sexual innocence became a standing joke:

> 'Tis true, indeed, we oft abuse him,
>   Because he bends to no man;
> But slander's self dares not accuse him
>   Of stiffness to a woman

or:

> Though big with mathematic pride
> By me this axiom is denied;
> I can't conceive, upon my soul,
> My parts are equal to the *whole*.(1)

---

(1) 'Epigrams on the Immaculate Boy', printed with *The Rolliad:* see no. 99.

This innocence also contributed to the suggestion about him of one-sidedness, if not incompleteness and abnormality, and to the view that his talents were entirely verbal, with no real creativity or constructive power behind his astonishing fluency of speech.

His ability as a speaker was indeed phenomenal. He spoke 'with the same deliberation and fluency as if he were reading a book. There was never a moment's hesitation for a word: the emphasis was always correct and beautiful, because it served to render the longest sentences intelligible'.(2) Yet his speeches were made without the least preparation. In fact, Pitt helped establish a parliamentary fashion for speeches lasting over three hours (previously, even budget speeches had lasted little more than one) and his mastery of words, even in his earliest days as Chancellor of the Exchequer in Shelburne's ministry, was the principal reason why George III first asked him to form a government when only 23.

Though, within the British political system, it was necessary for Pitt to maintain his position by keeping the support of the House of Commons, he resembled the other European chief ministers of his day in that his power ultimately derived from being approved and nominated by the king. The support of a large number of M.P.s depended in fact on his identification with the king, and when, in June 1803, during his temporary withdrawal from office, he attempted to divide the House of Commons against Henry Addington, the then prime minister, he received the support of only 55 M.P.s. Though George III relied on Pitt's control of the House of Commons, they were never on easy and intimate terms. A disagreement on the question of relaxing the penal laws against Roman Catholics in Ireland became the occasion of Pitt's resignation from office in February 1801, and thereafter George III seems to have regarded Pitt and his style of government with considerable suspicion. One may assume that theirs had always been a marriage of convenience.

---

(2) P. C. Scarlett, *A Memoir of the Right Honourable James, First Lord Abinger.* (London, 1877), 57.

In his official contacts, Pitt was extraordinarily stiff, frigid and distant, but within a small circle of mainly younger men he was willing to unbend and show off unsuspected gifts of wit and high spirits, and to the very end he exhibited a young man's optimism and openness to impressions. He seems almost never to have forgiven a political betrayal, or attempts at political independence, unless for some further purpose of politics, and he seems not to have forgiven Shelburne simply for having placed him under an obligation by appointing him to his first ministerial office in 1782; but he showed the more impetuous side of his character in accepting a challenge from George Tierney, whom he had insulted in the House of Commons. The two men, both hopeless pistol shots, fought a duel on Putney Heath on 27 May 1798, at that time an unprecedented event in the career of a prime minister, though the Duke of Wellington was to do likewise over thirty years later. Pitt was also a famous drinker, and in his early days as prime minister is alleged to have appeared drunk even in the House of Commons.

Despite the vast demands on his time he seems to have read widely and to have had a genuine interest in new ideas, including those of the economists Adam Smith and Thomas Malthus. Though in the 1790s, in the aftermath of the French Revolution, he sponsored the repression of lower-class reform associations in Britain, in the 1780s he had identified himself with the campaign for Parliamentary Reform and undoubtedly had a long-term interest in modernising the state institutions of the country, however much he sacrificed this interest to expediency and to his own tenure of power. One of his most important relationships was with William Wilberforce, who, as well as leading the campaign for the abolition of the Slave Trade, was the parliamentary spokesman of the emergent middle-class interest, with a commitment to institutional reform and probity and purity in public administration. Wilberforce never accepted government office and eventually joined in the parliamentary attack on Henry Dundas, Viscount Melville, formerly one of Pitt's closest ministerial colleagues and a man who Wilberforce had long regarded as a corrupting influence on

Pitt. Melville's impeachment for conniving at financial irregularities as Treasurer of the Navy was one of the circumstances which darkened the last months of Pitt's life, though for some time their association had been largely one of business.

Though George III appointed Pitt prime minister in late 1783 in order to counter the attempts of Charles James Fox and the Whigs to impose a stranglehold on the government system, the crisis in parliament and government was only part of a much wider *malaise* resulting from the nation's defeat in the War of American Independence. The first nine years of Pitt's government were a vital period of national recuperation and reconstruction. Pitt's policies restored the government's financial position, his reduction (1784) and simplification (1787) of various customs duties assisted the country's economic recovery, and his somewhat minor attempts to cut down on government sinecures and his espousal of parliamentary reform helped restore public confidence in the administrative system. From 1788 onwards a more aggressive foreign policy marked a sense of Britain's having lived down the disgrace of losing the American colonies and of having extricated itself from the diplomatic isolation of 1780–1782.

A belated, and in retrospect very ambiguous instance of Pitt's reformist tendencies, was his promotion of the legislative Union of Great Britain and Ireland. Though the immediate occasion for this measure was the Irish Rebellion of 1798, it had been evident since the 1780s that an independent legislature in Dublin posed serious problems of policy co-ordination and that the legal exclusion from public life of the Roman Catholic majority of the population (including even part of the titled nobility and some of the most dynamic elements of the Dublin bourgeoisie) was not only a fundamental weakness, and a profitless exclusion of potential talent from government service, but also gave assistance to disloyal elements amongst the Protestant minority. The legislative Union, by establishing control over Ireland of a United Kingdom Parliament dominated by Englishmen (and Protestants), was intended by Pitt as a preliminary to restoring the civil rights of the Irish Catholics, with the religious tests then existing probably being replaced by a system of loyalty oaths which would continue to disenfranchise many Catholics but would also disenfranchise many of the equally disaffected but hitherto legally emancipated Protestants. George III's objection to giving up the religious tests meant that, in the event, the Union simply reinforced Catholic discontent in Ireland, which was certainly not Pitt's intention.

After Britain was drawn into the war against Revolutionary France in 1793, Pitt the reconstructor gave way to Pitt the war leader. He had no original ideas on strategy and—what was probably more important at this stage—no appreciation of the kind of administrative and organisational reforms which were required to make the British armed forces, particularly the Army, more effective. He himself confessed, 'I distrust extremely any Ideas of my own on Military Subjects'.(3) He was also consistently let down by his European allies. His mismanagement of the war was not entirely his fault. Two of his Secretaries of State, Henry Dundas in the War and Colonial Department and Lord Grenville in the Foreign Department, were at least as responsible as Pitt for the policies that went adrift, though given the strategic options of the time it is not clear what kind of policies might have been guaranteed greater success. Pitt's prime individual responsibility, as First Lord of the Treasury and Chancellor of the Exchequer, was to pay for the war; that is, raising money not only for Britain's own military expenditure but also for the foreign subsidies which were an important though not very effective part in Britain's alliance policy. Initially, Pitt showed extraordinary virtuosity in raising loans on the London money market but after the financial crisis of 1797, he began to give more attention to new forms of taxation, though his initial attempt at Income Tax in 1798 was less successful in its original form than that later devised by his successor Addington.

---

(3) Lewis Melville, ed., *The Windham Papers*, 2 vols. (London, 1913), I: 246. Pitt to Windham, 21 September 1794.

Introduction 7

Addington's most important and most controversial achievement during Pitt's withdrawal from government, 1801–1804, was to make peace with France. When, inevitably, war broke out again, Pitt drilled his Volunteer regiment at Walmer Castle till growing public clamour for his return to office led him to oppose Addington in parliament. When Addington resigned in May 1804, Pitt was under considerable pressure to establish a coalition ministry which would include his old adversary Fox. This was unacceptable to the king; and a number of Pitt's former cabinet colleagues, including his cousin Lord Grenville, refused to return to office with him when he formed his second ministry. Pitt's 1804–1806 government was thus rather more of a one-man affair than his earlier tenure of office, and even more than in the 1790s he appeared the great champion of European resistance to French aggression. 'England has saved herself by her exertions, and will, as I trust, save Europe by her example', he announced after Nelson's spectacular victory over a Franco-Spanish fleet off Cape Trafalgar; 'Roll up that map: it will not be wanted these ten years', he exclaimed in agony when the news arrived of the French victory at Austerlitz over the Russo-Austrian coalition which he had helped finance. The timing of events was suitably dramatic, for shortly after the news of Austerlitz, he took to his death bed.

Pitt died at 4.30 a.m. on 23 January 1806. One future prime minister wrote, 'The sun is indeed set, and what can now follow, but the blackest night!'(4) Pitt had suffered intermittently since his teens from digestive disorders and gout. Partly encouraged by medical advice, he had kept himself going by heavy drinking and his death was almost certainly caused by alcoholism, involving cirrhosis of the liver and possibly also renal failure and gastric ulcers. His last words have been variously reported as, 'Oh my country! How I leave my country!' and 'I think I could eat one of Bellamy's veal pies'.

---

(4) British Library Add. 43337 f 2 'Memorabilia Politica' c. 25 January 1806, by the Earl of Aberdeen.

Chronology of Significant Events in the Life of William Pitt

1759—28 May	WILLIAM PITT born at Hayes, Kent, son of Hester (née Grenville) and William Pitt, M.P., Secretary of State for the Southern Department and Leader of the House of Commons, afterwards 1st Earl of Chatham
1773—26 April	matriculated at Pembroke Hall, later Pembroke College, Cambridge, having previously studied only at home; went into residence October 1773, proceeded M.A. Spring 1776
1776— 4 July	DECLARATION OF INDEPENDENCE AT PHILADELPHIA
1777—28 January	admitted at Lincoln's Inn—i.e. for qualification as a lawyer
1778—11 May	father died, leaving Pitt c.£600 a year income payable by his older brother, John, 2nd Earl of Chatham
1780—12 June	called to the Bar—i.e. registered as a practising trial lawyer
—September	stood unsuccessfully as parliamentary candidate for Cambridge University; elected at Appleby through influence

	of Sir James Lowther, afterwards 1st Earl of Lonsdale
1781—23 January	took seat in the House of Commons, adhering to the faction of the Earl of Shelburne
—26 February	delivered maiden speech in favour of economical reform
1782—12 April	BRITAIN SUES FOR PEACE IN AMERICAN WAR
— 6 July	appointed Chancellor of the Exchequer in Shelburne's administration
1783—24 March	on Shelburne's resignation asked by king to form a government: refused and resigned his place 31 March
—19 December	appointed First Lord of Treasury (i.e. Prime Minister) and Chancellor of the Exchequer
1784—March–April	fought general election, winning landslide victory against Charles James Fox and Lord North, and being elected M.P. for Cambridge University
1785—18 April	proposed motion in House of Commons for Parliamentary Reform
1786—26 May	secured enactment of the Sinking Fund to reduce the National Debt
—26 September	achieved further success with signing of Commercial Treaty with France
1788—November, to February 1789	successfully resisted Foxite attempt to establish a Regency during the temporary mental derangement of George III
1789—14 July	STORMING OF BASTILLE IN FRANCE MARKED BEGINNING OF THE FRENCH REVOLUTION
1790—May to October	conducted diplomatic campaign against Spain in Nootka Sound crisis

Chronology

1791— February to July	conducted unsuccessful diplomatic campaign against Russia in Oczakov crisis; appointed Lord Grenville Foreign Secretary in place of Duke of Leeds
1793— 1 February	FRENCH DECLARATION OF WAR
1794—11 July	recruited the Duke of Portland, Earls Spencer and Fitzwilliam and William Windham, leaders of the so-called Portland Whigs, to his cabinet
1797—26 February	forced by financial crisis to suspend cash payments (i.e. place currency on fiduciary basis in place of Gold Standard)
—15 April	ROYAL NAVY MUTINIED AT SPITHEAD, FOLLOWED BY MUTINY AT THE NORE 12 MAY—THE DARKEST DAYS OF PITT'S REGIME
—July to September	conducted, through Lord Malmesbury, peace negotiation with France at Lille
1798—23 May	REBELLION BROKE OUT IN IRELAND
—27 May	fought duel with George Tierney on Putney Heath
1800— 8 May	secured agreement of British Parliament to Legislative Union with Ireland
1801— 3 February	resigned office after disagreement with George III on Irish Roman Catholic issue; Addington, the new Prime Minister, shortly afterwards renewed peace negotiations with France
1803— 3 June	attempted, just over 2 weeks after resumption of war with France, to establish personal leadership of the

	House of Commons in defiance of Addington
1804— 7 May	agreed to form new government, though unable to secure participation of Lord Grenville, Earl Spencer or William Windham
—23 December	persuaded Addington to join cabinet; the latter resigned again 4 July 1805
1806—23 January	died at Bowling Green House, Putney
—22 February	ceremonially interred at Westminster Abbey

I. Unpublished Personal Papers

**indicates source of special importance

A. Great Britain

The National Register of Archives, Quality House, Quality Court, Chancery Lane, London WC2A 1HP, has detailed catalogues of most of the following collections and has up-to-date information on conditions of access to collections still in private hands. A microfiche index, giving in some instances more information but not yet covering all the relevant collections, has been published by Chadwyck-Healey Ltd. of Cambridge under the title *National Inventory of Documentary Sources in the United Kingdom* and is available in several research libraries in the U.S.A.

Cambridge
1. Pembroke College, Cambridge CB2 IRF
   Some material relating to Pitt's residence in college as an undergraduate, including some early letters; also reminiscences of him by Elizabeth Tomline, wife of his tutor—later his secretary—George Pretyman, later Tomline.
2. Cambridge University Library, West Road, Cambridge CB3 9DR
   Copies of about 4,000 letters received by Pitt 1786–1805.

Carlisle
3. Cumbria Record Office, The Castle, Carlisle CA3 8UR
   (Lonsdale Papers) A bundle of letters from Pitt to the 1st and 2nd Earls of Lonsdale, the most important of which have been printed by the Historical Manuscripts Commission, see no. 35.

Edinburgh
4. Scottish Record Office, General Register House, Edinburgh EH1 3YY
   (a) (Buccleuch Papers) Some letters from Pitt to Duke of Buccleuch 1787–1804.
   (b) (Hope of Luffness Papers) Some letters of Pitt to General Sir Alexander Hope, mainly regarding defence against invasion, 1803–1805.
   (c) (Melville House Muniments) Several important letters from Pitt to Henry Dundas 1794 and 1801–1805 in GD 51/1; a memo by Pitt c.1800 in GD 51/16/99.

Exeter
5. Devon Record Office, Castle Street, Exeter, Devon EX4 3PQ
   (a) (Sidmouth Papers) About 60 letters from Pitt to Henry Addington, his successor as prime minister, 1786–1803, the majority printed in George Pellew's biography of Addington, see no. 55.
   (b) (Simcoe Papers) 6 letters of Pitt to General John G. Simcoe, governor of San Domingo, 1796–1797.

Ipswich
6. Suffolk Record Office, County Hall, St Helen's Street, Ipswich IP4 2JS
   (Pretyman Papers) 80 letters from Pitt to George Pretyman Tomline, his tutor at Cambridge and later his secretary, 1774–1805.

Keele

7. Keele University Library, Keele, Staffordshire ST5 5BG (Sneyd Papers) 5 letters from Pitt to Lord Auckland on Irish affairs 1797–1799.

Leeds

8. Leeds Central Library (Archives Dept.), Chapleton Road, Sheepscar, Leeds LS7 3AD
   (Canning or Harewood Papers) Several letters from Pitt to George Canning 1792–1805.
   (Canning's correspondence with his wife, in the same collection, is a vital source for the study of Pitt and his associates during the same period.)

London

9. British Library (Department of Manuscripts), Great Russell Street, London WC1B 3DG
   (a) Add. 7979 2 letters to Comte Joseph de Puisaye, 1794–1795.
   (b) Add. 9344 2 letters to George Jackson, 1784 and 1790.
   (c) Add. 34420–34456 and Add. 34461 (Auckland Papers) over 100 letters from Pitt to Lord Auckland 1785–1804, the majority printed in G. Hogge's edition of Auckland's *Journal and Correspondence*, see no. 40.
   (d) Add. 35127 3 letters from Pitt to Arthur Young 1793.
   (e) Add. 35192 (Bridport Papers) 6 letters from Pitt to Admiral Lord Bridport 1782–1800.
   (f) **Add. 35424, Add. 35641 (Hardwicke Papers) several letters from Pitt to Earl Hardwicke on general political matters 1784–1805; Add. 35684–35685 several letters from Pitt to Hardwicke regarding Cam-

bridgeshire (of which Hardwicke was Lord Lieutenant); Add. 35706, Add. 35709–35710, Add. 35750–35751, Add. 35753–35757, Add. 35759–35761 Pitt's correspondence with Hardwicke on Irish affairs.
(g) Add. 37282–37283, Add. 37309 (Wellesley Papers) 5 letters from Pitt to the Marquis Wellesley 1800–1806.
(h) **Add. 37844 (Windham Papers) about 50 letters from Pitt 1792–1802 (mainly on war policy) and draft replies, about a dozen printed in [Lewis Melville ed.] *The Windham Papers,* see no. 42.
(i) Add. 38192 (Liverpool Papers) correspondence with the 1st Earl of Liverpool 1784–1801.
(j) Add. 38571 (Liverpool Papers) correspondence with Lord Hawkesbury, later 2nd Earl of Liverpool 1804.
(k) Add. 38735, Add. 38759 (Huskisson Papers) a letter from Pitt to Huskisson c. 1798 and a memo in Pitt's hand c.1802.
(l) Add. 40862 (Ripon Papers) 2 letters from Pitt to Lord Hobart 1793, 1803.
(m) Add. 41345 (Melville Papers) 2 letters from Pitt to Henry Dundas 1798, 1805.
(n) Add. 41694 (Willis Papers) 2 letters from Pitt to Rev. Dr. Thomas Willis 1801.
(o) Add. 41855 (Thomas Grenville Papers) 2 letters from Pitt to Thomas Grenville 1795.
(p) Add. 42772 (Rose Papers) correspondence, including items dealing with Pitt's personal financial affairs, 1783–1805; more than 20 of the letters from Pitt to Rose are printed in Rose's *Diaries and Correspondence,* see no. 39; there are also 2 letters from Pitt to the 1st Marquis of Stafford 1788 and 3 to Earl Gower, later 2nd Marquis of Stafford 1790–1803.
(q) Add. 43229 (Aberdeen papers) 4 letters from Pitt to Earl of Aberdeen 1801–1805 (Add. 43337 is Aber-

deen's 'Memorabilia Politica' dealing with the period of Pitt's death).

(r) Add. 45040 (supplementary Hardwicke Papers) 6 letters from Pitt to C.P. Yorke 1801–1804.

(s) Add. 46491 and Add. 46519 (Auckland Papers) further letters from Pitt to Lord Auckland 1785–1801; see also Add. 59704, the originals of Pitt's correspondence with Auckland, 1797, regarding the Hon. Miss Eleanor Eden, which was printed by the Earl of Rosebery in 1900 (see no. 45).

(t) **Add. 58906–58909 (Dropmore Papers) large number of letters from Pitt to Lord Grenville, his cousin and closest political confederate, 1783–1804. This is easily the largest and qualitatively the most important collection of Pitt's letters: the majority have been printed by the Historical Manuscripts Commission, see no. 33. Add. 59070–59071 contains some additional letters from Pitt to Grenville on Dutch affairs in the 1780s.

(u) Eg. 2182 3 letters from Pitt to John Douglas, Bishop of Carlisle and later of Salisbury 1788–1798.

(v) Eg. 3498 (Leeds Papers) 68 letters from Pitt to the Duke of Leeds, Foreign Secretary till 1791, and copies of the replies 1784–1791; also 1 letter from Pitt in Eg. 3506.

(w) Althorp Papers (not yet incorporated into main collection) 54 letters from Pitt to Earl Spencer 1783–1804, mainly relating to Spencer's term as First Lord of the Admiralty 1794–1801.

10. British Library of Political Science, London School of Economics, 10 Portugal Street, London WC2A 2HD

(Hammond Papers) 5 letters from Pitt to Lord Hawkesbury (later 2nd Earl of Liverpool) 1801–1802, and 4 from Pitt to George Hammond.

11. Historical Manuscripts' Commission, Quality House, Quality Court, Chancery Lane, London WC2A 1HP

(Eldon Papers, in possession of Lieutenant Colonel H.E. Scott) 27 letters from Pitt to Lord Chancellor Eldon 1804 and n.d., a third of them published in H. Twiss's biography of Eldon, see no. 59—it is necessary to apply to the Secretary of the Historical Manuscripts Commission to arrange access to this collection.

12. Public Record Office, Ruskin Ave., Kew, Surrey TW9 4DU
    (a) ** P.R.O. 30/8/101–363 (Chatham Papers) The principal surviving Pitt family archive—generally rather disappointing. It consists mainly of letters *to* Pitt (e.g. P.R.O. 30.8/103–194 and P.R.O. 30/8/264–271). P.R.O. 30/8/101 consists of letters from Pitt to members of his family (including 4 dating from his childhood) and to the King and Queen; P.R.O. 30/8/102 consists of about 100 letters from Pitt to various (often relatively unimportant) correspondents. P.R.O. 30/8/195–198 consists of notes, letterbooks and memoranda. P.R.O. 30/8/325 consists of letters from Pitt on Irish matters. Other classes include important *official* papers on finances &c. The whole collection is excellently indexed.
    (b) P.R.O. 30/29/384; 13 letters from Pitt to 1st Marquis of Stafford 1785–1803 and 3 to Stafford's younger son, Lord Granville Leveson Gower.
    (c) P.RO. 30/58/7 (Dacres Adams Papers) Notes from Pitt 1804–1805 regarding appointments, forwarding instructions for mails, books to be bought, and a verse translation from Horace. William Dacres Adams was Pitt's private secretary 1804–1806.
    (d) P.R.O. 30/70 (Hoare or Pitt Papers) Another fragment of the Pitt family archive; about 80 letters *to* Pitt.
N.B. The official papers produced by the Treasury during Pitt's nineteen years as First Lord of the Treasury and Chancellor of the Exchequer are also, of course, deposited in the Public Record Office but from the

mode in which government business was conducted in that period, they do not provide a source for the study of Pitt's personal role in financial policy.

Maidstone

13. Kent Archive Office, County Hall, Maidstone, Kent ME14 1XQ
    (a) (Amherst Papers) 2 letters from Pitt to Lord Amherst 1791, 1795.
    (b) (Pratt Papers) 21 letters from Pitt to Earl Camden 1784–1804; also an important memoir by Earl Camden on Pitt's resignation, printed in an article by Richard Willis in B.I.H.R., see no. 239.
    (c) (Sackville of Knole Papers) 19 items of correspondence between Pitt and the Duke of Dorset, ambassador to France till 1789, mainly the latter's requests and complaints.
    (d) (Stanhope Papers) Various letters from Pitt to members of the Stanhope family (Pitt's sister married the 3rd Earl Stanhope) including 18 letters to Lord Mahon 1802–1806 mainly about the latter's appointment as Lieutenant of Dover Castle. Classes S5/O9 and S5/O10 contain some notes and memos by Pitt on government business; S5/C46 is the Mss of Laurentius, a tragedy written by Pitt c. 1772–1773 (a scholarly edition is currently being prepared for publication); S5/C53 includes an undated translation from Tacitus and S5/C58 contains a sample of his hair which, as may still be seen today, was auburn.

Manchester

14. John Rylands Library, University of Manchester, Manchester M3 3EH
    (a) (Crawford Papers) Some letters from Pitt to Lord Muncaster.

(b) Catalogue, with some extracts, of Pitt's correspondence compiled by W. E. Tomline in 1834, and 60 letters of Henry Dundas to Pitt 1793–1805.
(c) Copies of George III's correspondence with Pitt.
(d) Papers relating to East Indian Affairs, partly by Pitt.

Northallerton

15. North Yorkshire Record Office, County Hall, Northallerton DL7 8SG
    (a) (Bolton Papers) Correspondence with Thomas Orde, later Lord Bolton, and also with the Duke of Rutland, concerning Irish affairs 1784–1787, partly published by Lord Ashbourne in his *Pitt,* see no. 36.
    (b) (Wyvill Papers) Correspondence with the Rev. Christopher Wyvill on Parliamentary Reform, published in Pitt's own lifetime by Wyvill, see no. 53.

Northampton

16. Northamptonshire Record Office, Delapre Abbey, Northampton NN4 9AW
    (Milton Mss) 3 letters from Pitt to Richard Burke, also some to Earl Fitzwilliam.

Nottingham

17. Manuscripts Department, Nottingham University, University Park, Nottingham NG7 2RD
    (Portland Papers) 16 letters from Pitt to the Duke of Portland 1784–1795.

Oakham

18. Barham Court, Exton Park, Oakham, Leics. LE15 8NN
    (Private family papers of present Earl of Gainsborough:

apply in writing) 9 letters from Pitt to Sir Charles Middleton, later Lord Barham 1787–1805.

Sheffield

19. Sheffield Central Library, Surrey Street, Sheffield S1 1XZ

    (Wentworth Woodhouse Mss) 10 letters from Pitt to Richard and Edmund Burke 1782–1795.

Stafford

20. Staffordshire Record Office, County Buildings, Eastgate Street, Stafford, ST16 2LZ

    (Sutherland Papers) 6 letters from Pitt to Earl Gower, later 1st Marquis of Stafford 1794–1800 and 1 letter to Earl Gower, later 2nd Marquis of Stafford 1802.
21. Sandon Hall, Stafford ST18 ODH

    (Private family papers of present Earl of Harrowby: apply in writing) 34 letters from Pitt to Lord Harrowby 1785–1806; also copies of material from Pretyman Papers.

Trowbridge

22. Wiltshire Record Office, County Hall, Trowbridge BA14 8JG

    (Herbert Papers) Some correspondence of Pitt with the Earl of Pembroke.

Whitchurch

23. Gredington, Whitchurch, Shropshire SY13 3DH

    (Private family papers of present Lord Kenyon: apply in writing) 14 letters from Pitt to Lord Chief Justice Kenyon 1784–1796; these have been printed by the Historical Manuscripts Commission, see no. 34.

Winchester

24. Hampshire Record Office, 20 Southgate Street, Winchester SO23 9EF
    (Wickham Papers) Notes by Pitt concerning insurrectionary plots in Ireland 1798–1799.

Windsor

25. Royal Archives, Windsor Castle, Berks
    Though access is usually given to the Royal Archives in the case of *bona fide* researchers, no catalogue of this huge and sometimes somewhat disordered archive has been prepared, and one would be well recommended to rely on the exhaustive editions of *The Later Correspondence of George III* and *The Correspondence of George, Prince of Wales, 1770–1812* prepared by Arthur Aspinall, see nos. 37 and 38. These include Pitt's letters to the King and Prince of Wales. If in doubt, write to Her Majesty's Librarian, Windsor Castle, Berks., SL4 1NJ.

B. United States of America

Ann Arbor, Michigan

26. William L. Clements Library, University of Michigan, Ann Arbor, Michigan 48109
    196 letters from Pitt to various correspondents including Henry Dundas, George Rose, Lord Sydney, the Marquis Wellesley 1780–1805; also 76 letters from Pitt's parents and brothers.

Cleveland, Ohio

27. Cleveland Public Library, 325 Superior Avenue, Cleveland, Ohio 44114
    (John G. White Collection) Some letters from Pitt on Indian affairs c.1798–1800.

Durham, North Carolina

28. William R. Perkins Library, Duke University, Durham, North Carolina 27706
    (a) (Pitt Papers) About 100 items of correspondence 1773–1804 collected after Pitt's death from his country retreat at Holwood.
    (b) There are also odd letters from Pitt in classes 1641 (Lord Auckland) 1913 (Stephen Fuller) 2126 (Sir William Grant) 2835 (Earl of Liverpool) and 5726 (William Wilberforce).

II. Published Compilations of Original Papers
(See also Section III)

**indicates source of special importance

A. Historical Manuscripts Commission Reports

29. *5th Report,* p. 212, prints excerpts and paraphrases of 4 letters from Pitt to 1st Marquis of Stafford 1784–1800, now in Staffordshire Record Office.
30. *12th Report* appendix IX (Mss of W.N. Saumarez Smith) 1 letter from and several to Pitt 1785–1790, originally in possession of Joseph Smith, Pitt's private secretary.
31. *Report on the Manuscripts of Earl Bathurst preserved at Cirencester Park* 1923.
    Includes 13 letters from Pitt to Earl Bathurst 1797–1806, also 3 from Pitt to the Duke of Richmond 1794–1795.
32. *Report on the Manuscripts of the Earl of Carlisle preserved at Castle Howard* 1897.
    Includes 4 (not very important) letters from Pitt to the Earl of Carlisle 1793–1804.
33. ***Report on the Manuscripts of J.B. Fortescue, Esq., preserved at Dropmore* 10 vols. 1892–1927. (normally cited as *HMC Dropmore Mss*) contains in vols. 1–7 most

of the letters now in the British Library Add. 58906–58909.
34. *Report on the Manuscripts of Lord Kenyon preserved at Gredington* 1894.
    Prints the 14 letters from Pitt still preserved at Gredington, Whitchurch.
35. *Report on the Manuscripts of the Earl of Lonsdale* 1893, prints 24 letters from Pitt to Sir James Lowther, later 1st Earl of Lonsdale, and to his heir, Viscount Lowther, 1783–1805, from the bundle now at Cumberland Record Office, Carlisle.

B. Other Collections
(in alphabetical order of editors)

36. Ashbourne, Edward 1st Lord, ed. *Pitt, some chapters of his Life and Times* London 1898.
    Extensive selection of correspondence from Chatham, Bolton, Tomline and Stanhope papers.
37. **Aspinall, Arthur, ed. *The Later Correspondence of George III* 5 vols. Cambridge, 1962–1970.
    Prints a large number of letters from Pitt, mainly from the Royal Archives.
38. ———. *The Correspondence of George, Prince of Wales, 1770–1812* 8 vols. London, 1963–1971.
    Prints a number of letters from Pitt to the Prince of Wales, now preserved in the Royal Archives.
39. Harcourt, L.V., ed. *The Diaries and Correspondence of the Right Hon. George Rose* 2 vols. London, 1860.
    Prints more than 20 letters from Pitt to Rose.
40. Hogge, George, ed. *The Journal and Correspondence of William, Lord Auckland* 4 vols. London, 1861–1862.
    Prints about 70 letters from Pitt now in the Auckland Papers in the British Library.
41. Londonderry, Charles, 3rd Marquis of, ed. *Memoir and Correspondence of Viscount Castlereagh* 12 vols. London, 1848–1853.
    Later volumes entitled *Correspondence, Despatches*

and Other Papers; prints about half a dozen letters from Pitt to Lord Castlereagh.

42. [Melville, Lewis, ed.] *The Windham Papers* 2 vols. London, 1913.

    Prints about a dozen letters from Pitt to Windham from amongst those now in the British Library.

43. Rose, J. Holland. *Pitt and Napoleon: Essays and Letters* London, 1912.

    Includes an extensive selection from the Chatham and Tomline papers.

44. Rosebery, Archibald, 5th Earl of, ed. *Pitt and Wilberforce* printed for private circulation 1897.

    Prints correspondence of Pitt and William Wilberforce, the anti-slavery campaigner, 1782–1804, and a 'Sketch of Mr. Pitt' written by Wilberforce.

45. ———. *Letters relating to the Love Episode of William Pitt together with an Account of his Health by his Physician Sir Walter Farquhar* printed for private circulation 1900.

    Prints correspondence of Pitt and Lord Auckland 1797 regarding the former's interest in the latter's daughter, the Hon. Miss Eleanor Eden. Pitt soon gave up the idea of marrying her because he was up to the eyes with private debts. The originals are in the British Library Add. 59704.

46. Stanhope, Philip Henry, 5th Earl, (known in his father's lifetime as Lord Mahon) ed. *Correspondence between the Right Hon. William Pitt and Charles, Duke of Rutland, Lord Lieutenant of Ireland 1781–1787.* Printed for private circulation, 1842.

    Reprinted for publication, with 8 page introduction by the then Duke of Rutland, Edinburgh and London 1890.

47. ———. *Secret Correspondence connected with Mr. Pitt's Return to Office in 1804* London, 1852.

    Prints Pitt's letters to Lords Melville and Eldon March–May 1804; these were later reprinted in Stanhope's biography of Pitt, see no. 58.

48. ———. *Notes and Extracts of Letters referring to Mr. Pitt and Walmer Castle, 1801–1806*. Printed for private circulation 1866.
    Prints letters from Stanhope papers.
49. ———. *Miscellanies* Vol. II. London, 1872.
    Prints letters from Pitt to Earl Temple, 1783, to Sir Walter Farquhar (his doctor) and to Charles, 3rd Earl Stanhope, his brother-in-law.
50. Taylor, William Stanhope and Pringle, John Henry, ed. *Correspondence of William Pitt, Earl of Chatham* 4 vols. London, 1838–1840.
    Prints 7 letters from Pitt to his father 1773–1777 and 5 to his mother 1774–1778.
51. Wilberforce, A.M., ed. *Private Papers of William Wilberforce* London, 1897.
    Prints 24 letters from Pitt to Wilberforce 1782–1804
52. Wilberforce, Robert Isaac and Samuel, ed. *The Correspondence of William Wilberforce* 2 vols London, 1840.
    Prints 10 letters from Pitt to Wilberforce 1783–1803
53. Wyvill, Christopher, ed. *Correspondence of the Rev. C. Wyvill with the Rt. Hon. W. Pitt* Two parts, Newcastle, 1796–1797.
    Largely consists of Wyvill's letters to Pitt on the Parliamentary Reform issue but includes 7 short notes by Pitt, a memorandum by Pitt, and notes by Wyvill of 2 conversations with Pitt, 1782–1786. Reprinted in Wyvill's *Political Papers, chiefly respecting the Attempt of the County of York . . . to effect a Reformation of the Parliament of Great Britain* 6 vols. York 1794–1802.

III. Other Works Printing Letters from Pitt *in Extenso*

** *indicates source of special importance*

54. Black, Jeremy. 'An Unpublished Letter from William Pitt' *Durham University Journal* LXXVIII/2 (1984) p. 345–6. A letter from Pitt to his mother, the Countess of Chatham, discussing the preliminary terms for peace with France, 1801.
55. Pellew, George. *The Life and Correspondence of the Right Hon. Henry Addington, 1st Viscount Sidmouth* 3 vols. London, 1847.
    Prints 40 of Pitt's letters now preserved in the Sidmouth Papers in the Devon Record Office.
56. Phipps, Edmund. *Memoirs of the Political and Literary Life of Robert Plumer Ward, Esq.* 2 vols. London, 1850.
    Prints 4 letters from Pitt and many others from his political associates.
57. Rose, John Holland. 'Pitt and the Campaign of 1793 in Flanders' *English Historical Review* XXIV (1909) p. 744–749.
    Prints several letters from Sir James Murray preserved in the Chatham Papers in the Public Record Office, and one lengthy reply from Pitt.
58. **Stanhope, Philip Henry, 5th Earl. *Life of the Right*

Hon. William Pitt 4 vols. London, 1861–1862.

Prints many important letters from Pitt.

59. Twiss, Horace. *The Public and Private Life of Lord Chancellor Eldon, with Selections from his Correspondence* 3 vols. London, 1844.

    Prints 9 letters from Pitt 1804, also 1 from Pitt to Sir William Scott 1805.

60. Wilberforce, Robert Isaac and Samuel. *The Life of William Wilberforce* 5 vols. London, 1838.

    Prints about 10 letters from Pitt to Wilberforce 1784–1802 and contains important additional material on Pitt's earlier political career from William Wilberforce's journals.

IV. Speeches

At least eleven of Pitt's speeches in the House of Commons were published as pamphlets; that of 31 January 1799 outlining his proposals for the Legislative Union of Great Britain and Ireland exists in at least nine different editions.

The standard sources for Pitt's parliamentary speeches are:

61. (a) Cobett, W. ed. *The Parliamentary History of England, from the Earliest Period to the Year 1803* 36 vols. London, 1806–1820.
    (b) Cobbett, W. and Hansard, T.C. ed. *The Parliamentary Debates from the Year 1803 to the Present Time* 41 vols. London, 1812–1820.
    (c) Debrett, J. ed. *The Parliamentary Register* 2nd series, 45 vols. London, 1781–1796; 3rd series, 18 vols. London, 1797–1802; 4th series, 2 vols. London, 1803.

It should be noted, however, that Cobbett's *Parliamentary History,* though more generally available in research libraries than Debrett's *Parliamentary Register,* and though, in some senses, better laid-out, does not give such full or accurate reports of the debates. Condensed versions of many debates are given in *The Annual Register.*

62. [W.S. Hathaway, ed] *The Speeches of the Right Honourable William Pitt in the House of Commons* 4 vols. London, 1806 (and various later editions) is still the

fullest collected edition. Based on various sources, the reports are even fuller than in Debrett, but all Pitt's shorter interpellations and many of his financial speeches are not included.

Various extracts from the Hathaway edition have been published, of which the most readily available is as follows:

R. Coupland, ed. *The War Speeches of William Pitt the Younger* Oxford, 1915; 2nd edition 1916; 3rd edition 1940.

V. Published Writings of Pitt

Apart from his various published speeches—not corrected by Pitt personally—and the unpublished items preserved in the Public Record Office (Dacres Adams Papers) and the Kent Archives Office, Maidstone (Stanhope Papers), and of course, his private letters and memoranda, Pitt wrote almost nothing and only once put his name to a non-official publication:

63. A letter dated 29 October 1778 *The Annual Register* vol. 21 (1778) p. 257–261.
    Defending his father against the aspersions of Lord Mountstuart.

In 1797, some of his younger supporters, led by George Canning, established a weekly satirical review entitled *Anti-Jacobin; or Weekly Examiner*. This lasted less than a year, and is not to be confused with the much less interesting though more durable *Anti-Jacobin Review and Magazine* (1799–1821). Pitt contributed the following to the *Anti-Jacobin*—all the articles were anonymous:

64. (Prose)
    (a) article on Finance in No. 1 (20 Nov. 1797), p. 2.
    (b) article on Finance in No. 2 (27 Nov. 1797), p. 9–10; these two articles discuss the tripling of the Assessed Taxes and explicitly deny possession of any inside information.

(c) article on Finance in No. 3 (30 Nov. 1797), p. 19–20.
(d) article on Finance in No. 12 (29 Jan. 1798), p. 89–90; justifies government financial measures generally.
(e) article on Finance in No. 25 (30 April 1798), p. 193–194; discusses policy of loans and taxes.
(f) review of the session in No. 35 (2 July 1798), p. 273–276; this is actually an account of developments in the war with France since the previous autumn; the style of writing is strikingly concise and forceful, especially when compared to his orotund speeches.

(Poetry)

Pitt also supposedly wrote the last stanza of the 'Song by Rogero' in No. 30 (4 June 1798), p. 239:

> Sun, moon, and thou vain world, adieu
>   That kings and priests are plotting in:
> Here doom'd to starve on water gru-
> - el, never shall I see the U ——
>   - niversity of Gottingen
>   - niversity of Gottingen.

The British Library's copy of the *Anti-Jacobin* shelved at C.40 1.2 has contemporary annotations—it is believed by George Canning—giving most of these attributions: in addition a post-card pasted into this copy gives a second-hand report, naming Lord Grenville as authority, that Pitt also wrote 'The Choice', adapted from 'The Battle of Sabla' in Joseph Dacre Carlyle's *Specimens of Arabian Poetry* Cambridge, 1796, printed in No. 8 (1 January 1798), p. 61–62.

VI. Pamphlets Etc. Relating to Pitt

**indicates source of special interest

A. Satirical Attacks on Pitt

Pitt lived at a period when scabrous political satire was in fashion, and the extraordinarily early age at which he became Prime Minister, and speculation about his sex-life (or non-existence thereof) resulted in his being more viciously pilloried than almost any other Prime Minister before or since. He seems not to have cared in the least.

65. Adams, William. *Thoughts on the anti-monarchical tendency of the measures of the British Minister* London, 1796.
    An exercise in very labored sarcasm.
66. Baldpate, Grizzle [pseud.] *The Poll Tax, an Ode* London, 1795.
67. *Billy Brass: a political hudibrastic* London, 1785
    In verse.
68. [Bridge, J.?] *The tenth chapter of the acts of the Chancellor of the Exchequer* London, 1785.
    An attack on the Shop Tax: there is a copy in the Goldsmiths' Library, Senate House, Malet Street, London WC1E 7HU.

69. *The Chapter of the Acts of the Chancellor of the Exchequer* Salisbury, 1785.

    A broadsheet, not identical to the previous item which is 14 pages long; travesties of religious documents were a common satirical device of the period.

70. *Cheap Whisky; a familiar epistle to Mr. Pitt* London, 1796.

    In verse.

71. *The Christmas Tale, a poetical address and remembrance to the young ministry* London, 1784.

72. *A Contrast on Mr. Brothers and Mr. Pitt* 1800.

    Richard Brothers was a religious visionary, at that time confined as a lunatic.

73. *Copy of a Declaration and Articles subscribed by the members of administration* London, 1789.

    A spoof version of the Articles of Religion in the Prayer Book.

74. *A Creed for all good and loyal subjects who go to Saint Paul's on the 19th of December, 1797* [1797].

    A broadsheet, lampooning the General Thanksgiving ordered for 19 December 1797; also published as *Political Creed*.

75. *The Dispute of Mr. Pitt and Mr. Tiern-y* [1798].

    Verses on their duel.

76. *An Epistle from the Reverend William M--n, to the Right Hon. William Pitt* [1785].

    A satire showing the poet Mason petitioning the minister for the vacant Laureateship.

77. *The Extraordinary and Facetious History of the Immaculate Boy* 1785.

    Broadsheet, parody of William Cowper's ballad 'John Gilpin'.

78. *The Family Tale, or the story of Pitt, Fox and O'Connor* London, 1798.

    Arthur O'Connor was one of the United Irish leaders; Fox was the leader of the Whig opposition.

79. *A Full, true and particular Account of the Birth, Parentage and Education, Life, Character and Behaviour of that*

most notoriously notified Malefactor Willy Pitto who is to be executed in Effigy for his most horrid Crimes on the 5th of November next being the Anniversary of the Acquittal of Thomas Hardy [1795].

A penny broadsheet with a crude woodcut, of the type still circulated before the public execution of noted malefactors. Hardy had been prosecuted unsuccessfully for High Treason in 1794.

80. Meadley, G. W. *Two Pairs of Historical Portraits: Octavius Caesar and William Pitt: Rienzi and Buonaparte* London, 1821.

    A comparison of Octavius, later the Emperor Augustus, and Pitt, generally unfavourable to the latter.

81. *The Minister's A——* London, 1784.

    Broadsheet, in verse.

82. *The Minister, impregnable* London, 1790.

    In verse.

83. *Mustapha's Adoration of the Sublime Sultan Pittander Omnipotent* 1795. 3 parts, No. 3 entitled *Mustapha's Vision Addressed with Humble and Devout Adoration to the Sublime Sultan Pittander Omnipotent*.

    3 separate broadsheets something in the style of the Song of Solomon:

    > Fain would I bow me down and kiss thy hinder parts in testimony of my submission, but thy hinder parts are wanting; I would pour precious ointment on thy beard, but thou art without a chin

84. *Naked Truth: addressed to the people of England on the successful struggles of liberty. With a few gentle hints to a heaven-born minister* London, 1790.

85. Nergalsharezerneborabmagshamgar [pseud.] *The Book of the Wars of Westminster: from the fall of the Fox at the close of 1783, to the 20th day of the third month, 1784, on which William the Conqueror celebrated the third Grand Lent Festival, at the London* [1784].

36 pages in mock-biblical style, allegedly translated from the Ethiopian.
86. *The Petition at the sign of the Fox and Sour Plumbs* [1800?].
In verse, ridicules a petition for the dismissal of Pitt.
87. Pindar, Peter [pseud., i.e., John Wolcot]. *A Poetical Epistle to a Falling Minister* London, 1789.
88. ———. *A Letter to the most Insolent Man Alive* London, 1789.
89. ———. *More Money; or, Odes of Instruction to Mr. Pitt* London, 1792.
90. ———. *Hair Powder: a plaintive epistle to Mr. Pitt* London, 1795.
91. ———. *Out at Last! or the Fallen Minister* London, 1801: at least 6 editions.
92. ———. *Pitt to his Statue* London, 1802.
Dr John Wolcot was very well known in his day, under the pseudonym Peter Pindar, for his bitter satirical verse. If his attacks on Pitt were ever amusing, they must have dated badly.
93. *Pitt's Ghost, being an account of the death, and horrible apparition of the much lamented late Minister of State* [1795].
First published in *The Telegraph* 20, 21 and 24 August 1795, there are at least 6 progressively extended pamphlet editions, the first entitled, *Admirable Satire on the death, dissection, funeral procession and epitaph of Mr. Pitt,* and the 6th and longest, *A faithful narrative of the last illness, death, and interment of the Rt. Hon. W. Pitt. . . . with an account of the dreadful apparition in Downing Street.*
94. *Pitti-Clout and Dun-Cuddy. A political eclogue* [1795].
In verse.
95. *Pittpatche's Requisition!? Proclamation extraordinary? Given at our Court of Pandaemonium* [1795].
Penny broadsheet set out in imitation of an official proclamation.
96. *A Political Dictionary for the Guinealess Pigs, or a glos-*

Pamphlets Etc. Relating to Pitt 39

sary of Emphatical Words made use of by that Jewel of a Man, Deep Will [1790].
97. *Poor old England! Billy-Boy and the East India nabobs: or taxation for ever* [1784].
   A ballad; there is a copy in the Goldsmiths' Library, Senate House, Malet Street, London, WC1E 7HU
98. *The Reign of the English Robespierre* London, 1795.
   An 8 page polemic, 'Addressed to the Nation'.
99. ** [Joseph Richardson, Richard Tickell, French Laurence] *Criticisms of the Rolliad* Part One London, 1784, 9th edition 1795; Part Two 1785, 5th edition 1790; *Probationary Odes for the Laureateship* and *Political Eclogues* usually included from 1785; both parts together, plus *Probationary Odes, Political Eclogues* and additional squibs, appeared as a single volume 1795, 21st edition 1799.
   Consists of a mock serious scholarly critique with extracts of verse from a spoof epic poem about John Rolle, later Lord Rolle, one of Pitt's most loyal supporters. The verses were at one time justly famous: Pitt is described thus:

   Pert without fire, without experience sage,
   Young with more art than Sh——e glean'd from age
   . . . .
   In solemn dignity and sullen state
   This new *Octavius* rises to debate!

   Some of the other squibs pioneer techniques of political satire still in use today.
100. *The School for Scandal, a comedy in five acts, as it is performed by His Majesty's Servants* London, 1784.
   Sheridan's play *The School for Scandal* had been a great success in 1777.
101. Twisting, Tim. *The Pittiad; or Poetico-Political History of William the Second, in five cantos* London, 1785.
   There appears to be no copy of this 50 page poem in

any British library, though there is one in the library of the University of Illinois, Urbana. Not to be confused with Doll Common, *The Pittiad,* a 16 page quarto published in 1759 against Pitt's father, the later Earl of Chatham.
102. *Whig and no Whig, a political paradox* London 1789.
   A dialogue between William and Charles, i.e., Pitt and Fox.
103. *Wonderfull Exhibition! Positively the last Season of his Performing—Signor Gulielmo Pittachio, the Sublime Wonder of the World!!!* [1795].
   A penny broadsheet, set out like a playbill.

B. Other Pamphlets Dealing with Pitt
grouped according to topics, and including some articles in contemporary periodicals

Constitutional Crisis of 1783–1784

104. *A Letter to the Right Hon. W. Pitt from a Presbyterian of the Kirk of Scotland* [1784].
105. *Observations on the principles and tendency of the East India Bills proposed by the Right Honourable Charles James Fox and the Right Honourable William Pitt, with short sketches of their political character* London, 1784.

Parliamentary Reform

106. *A Letter to the Right Hon. W. Pitt on his Apostacy from the cause of Parliamentary Reform* London, 1792.

The War with France

107. *A Letter to the Right Hon. W. Pitt on the doctrines laid down by him respecting the introduction of foreign troops* London, 1794.
108. *A Letter to the Rt. Hon. W. Pitt on the present alarming Crisis of Public Affairs* London, 1796.

109. *The Merits of Mr. Pitt and Mr. Hastings in War and in Peace impartially stated* London, 1794.
110. Plummer, T. *The Inconsistencies of Mr. Pitt, on the subject of the war, and the present state of our commerce, considered, and fairly stated* London, 1797.
   (Copy in Goldsmiths' Library, Senate House, Malet Street, London WC1E 7HU).
111. *A Refutation of Mr. Pitt's alarming assertion . . . . . "That, unless the Monarchy of France be restored, the Monarchy of England will be lost"* London, 1794.
112. *Three Words to Mr. Pitt on the War and on the Peace* London, 1801.

Public Finance

113. Brutus [pseud.] *Cursory Remarks on Mr. Pitt's new tax of imposing a guinea per head on every person who wears hair powder* London, 1795.
114. Effingham, Earl of. *An Examination of Mr. Pitt's plan for diminishing the Public Debts by means of a sinking fund* London, 1787.
115. *A Letter, addressed to the Right Honourable, Lord Henry Petty wherein the general tendency of the principles of his great predecessor's financial administration are freely and plainly examined* Bristol, 1806.
   Petty became Chancellor of the Exchequer on Pitt's death in 1806.
116. *A Letter to the Right Honourable William Pitt on his conduct with respect to the loan concluded on the twenty-fifth of November last, and the suspicious circumstances attending that transaction* London, 1796.
   (Copy in Goldsmiths' Library)
117. *A Letter to the Right Honourable William Pitt . . . . on the conduct of the Bank directors; with cursory observations on Mr. Morgan's pamphlet, respecting the expence of the war, and the state of the National Debt* London, 1796.
118. Morgan, William. *Facts addressed to the serious atten-*

tion of the People of Great Britain respecting the expence of the war, and the state of the National Debt* London, 1796 (4 editions).

119. ———. *Additional Facts, addressed to the serious attention of the People of Great Britain respecting the expences of the war, and the state of the National Debt* London, 1796 (4 editions).

120. ———. *An Appeal to the People of Great Britain on the Present alarming state of the public finances and of public credit* London, 1797 (4 editions).

121. ———. *A Comparative View of the Public Finance from the beginning to the close of the late Administration* London, 1801.

> Morgan, an actuary, was convinced that Britain was being bankrupted by the war after 1793. There were a number of replies to his accusations, including the last 3 items in this section.

122. *A Protest against Mr Pitt's new Method of raising the supplies* London, 1797.

123. Stanhope, Charles, 3rd Earl. *Observations on Mr. Pitt's plan for the reduction of the National Debt* London, 1786.

124. [untitled sheet: begins] *The unusual Industry exerted to impress on the Public Mind a Persuasion that Mr. Pitt found the country in a flourishing, and left it in a ruinous state, has rendered it necessary, as an act of justice to his memory, that a few plain facts should be stated* [1806].

125. Vansittart, Nicholas. *An Inquiry into the State of the Finances of Great Britain; in answer to Mr. Morgan's Facts* London, 1796.

126. Wakefield, Daniel. *Observations on the credit and finances of Great Britain, in reply to the Thoughts of the Earl of Lauderdale and the Appeal of Mr. Morgan* London, 1797.

127. ———. *An Investigation of Mr. Morgan's Comparative View of the Public Finances from the beginning to the close of the close of the late Administration* London, 1801.

The State of the Poor

128. Howlett, John. *Examination of Mr. Pitt's Speech in the House of Commons, on Friday, February 12, 1796, relative to the condition of the Poor* London, 1796.

The Legislative Union with Ireland

Of a very large number of pamphlets dealing with this subject, the following relate somewhat more particularly to Pitt.

129. *The Conspiracy of Pitt and Co. detected in a Letter to the Parliament of Ireland. By one of the people* Dublin, 1799.
130. Drennan, William. *A Letter to the Right Honourable W. Pitt* Dublin, 1799.
131. ———. *Second Letter to the Right Honourable William Pitt* Dublin, 1799.

Pitt's First Administration Generally

132. *An Address to the Right Hon. W. Pitt . . . . . on some parts of his administration, occasioned by his proposal of the Triple Assessment in the House of Commons* London, 1797.
    Possibly by the poet T. J. Mathias.
133. *An Address to the Sovereign, on the Minister's conduct in rejecting the Petitions of the Lieutenants of the Royal Navy* London, 1788.
134. Beddoes, Thomas. *An Essay on the Public Merits of Mr. Pitt* London, 1796.
    A wide-ranging, cogent and elegant attack, 210 pages long, more a book than a pamphlet.
135. *Characters of the Right Hon. W. Pitt and R. B. Sheridan* Paris, 1804.
136. *Friendly Remarks upon some particulars of his Administration, in a letter to Mr. Pitt, by a Near Observer* London, 1796.
137. Gam, David, *Memoirs of the Administration of the Right*

Honourable William Pitt; or an inquiry into the causes and consequences of his conduct in respect to different departments, bodies and public individuals* London, 1797.
138. *A Hasty Sketch of Mr. Pitt's celebrated administration* London, 1800.
139. Horne Tooke, John. *Two Pairs of Portraits presented to all the Unbiassed Electors of Great-Britain; and especially the Electors of Westminster* London, 1788.
Draws parallels between Lord Holland and the Earl of Chatham and between their sons Charles James Fox and William Pitt; essentially an attack on Fox and almost an eulogy of Pitt. Six years later, Pitt had Horne Tooke charged with High Treason.
140. *The Opinion of an old Englishman: in which national honour and national gratitude are principally considered. Humbly offered to his countrymen and fellow citizens, on the resignation of the late Ministry* London, 1801.
141. Pasquin, Anthony. [pseud., i.e. John Williams.] *Legislative Biography; or, an Attempt to Ascertain the Merits and Principles of the Most Admired Orators of the British Senate* London, 1795.
Begins with 13 critical pages on Pitt.
142. *Sketches of the Right Honourable William Pitt and the Right Honourable Charles James Fox* [1800?].

Pitt's Relations with the Addington Ministry

The period of Pitt's retirement from office produced a notable crop of unusually weighty pamphlets discussing party politics, some of them by M.P.'s or other persons with confidential sources of information.

143. [Bentley, Thomas Richard.] *A Few Cursory Remarks upon the state of the parties during the Administration of the Rt. Hon. H. Addington. By a Near Observer* London, 1803.

Pamphlets Etc. Relating to Pitt 45

There were at least 9 editions of this government-inspired pamphlet.
144. ———. *A Reply of a Near Observer to some of the Answerers of the Cursory Remarks* London, 1804.
145. [Bisset, Robert.] *A Plain Reply to the Pamphlet calling itself "A Plain Answer", being a more fair state of the Question between the last and present Ministers* London, 1804.
146. [Courtenay, Thomas Peregrine.] *A Plain Answer to the misrepresentations contained in the Cursory Remarks of a near observer. By a more accurate observer.* London, 1803.
147. *Fitz-Albion's Letters to the Right Hon. William Pitt and the Right Hon. Henry Addington, on the subject of the Ministerial pamphlet entitled Cursory Remarks on the state of Parties.* London, 1803.
    (Copy in Goldsmiths' Library, Senate House, Malet Street, London WC1E 7HU).
148. *A Letter to Robert Ward Esq., M.P., occasioned by his pamphlet, intituled, a View of the relative situation of Mr. Pitt and Mr. Addington* London, 1804.
149. *Observations occasioned by the pamphlet called Cursory Remarks, or, A Comparative glance at the political merits of the Right Hon. H. Addington and W. Pitt* London, [1803].
150. *Thoughts recommendatory of a Coalition between the great Parliamentary leaders, in a letter to the author of 'A View of the Relative Situations of Mr. Pitt and Mr. Addington'* London, 1804.
151. *A Vindication of Mr. Pitt, for having moved to the previous question on the motion of Colonel Patten* London, 1804.
    (Copy in Goldsmiths' Library)
    Refers to Pitt's attempt, on 3 June 1803, to assert his leadership of the Commons in rivalry with the then prime minister, Henry Addington.
152. [Ward, Robert.] *A View of the Relative Situations of Mr.*

Pitt and Mr. Addington, previous to and on the night of Mr Patten's motion London, 1804.

Perhaps the most influential of these pamphlets, because written by a protégé of Viscount Lowther, the greatest borough patron of the day, and thought to express views shared by him and other great landlords who had formerly supported Pitt. Ward was M.P. for Cockermouth, one of the Lowther boroughs.

Pitt's Second Administration

153. *An Attempt to explain the late mysterious conduct of the Right Hon. William Pitt: with observations on some late political events* London, 1805.
154. Hamilton, Lord Archibald. *Thoughts on the formation of the late and present Administrations* London, 1804
    Lord Hamilton, a Foxite, was M.P. for Lanarkshire.
155. *A Reply to Lord A. Hamilton's Thoughts on the formation of the late and present Administrations.* London, 1804.

Tributes and Criticisms of Pitt after his Death

156. *An impartial account of the life and death of the Right Hon. William Pitt* Leeds, 1806.
    36 page pamphlet, very balanced, published and perhaps written by the Whig journalist, Edward Baines.
157. *An Inscription for the proposed Monument to Mr. Pitt* [1806].
    A broadsheet, signed WILKS.
158. [Jones, Stephen.] review of *Tomline's Speech on the character of the Right Hon. William Pitt* in *Monthly Review* vol. 53 (May–Aug. 1807) p. 81–92.
159. ———. review of Hathaway's collected edition of Pitt's speeches in *Monthly Review* vol. 58 (Jan.–April 1809), p. 402–417.
160. *A Letter to a Friend, occasioned by the death of the Right Hon. W. Pitt* London, 1806.
161. Plutarch [pseud.] *The Pilot that weather'd the storm. An*

attempt to record the political principles, sentiments and motives of the Right Hon. W. Pitt London, 1812.

162. Rose, George, *A Brief examination into the increase of the revenue, commerce and navigation of Great Britain, during the administration of the Rt. Hon. William Pitt . . . . . and a sketch of Mr. Pitt's character* London, 1806.

This is an edition of a work first published in 1792, with the sketch of Pitt's character added. Rose was Pitt's principal assistant in finance administration. This edition, though not particularly rare, is not in the British Library but is available in the Goldsmiths' Library.

163. Sharp, James. *A few Remarks, addressed to John Bernard Trotter, Esq., on the scandalous Attack made upon the Character of the Right Hon. William Pitt in his 'Memoirs of the latter years of the Right Hon. Charles James Fox'* London, 1812.

164. Tomline, George Pretyman. *A Speech on the Character of the Right Hon. William Pitt delivered at Trinity College Chapel Cambridge 17 December 1806* Cambridge, 1806.

Tomline was Pitt's tutor at Cambridge, later his private secretary, and finally his executor and biographer.

165. *A Vindication of the character of the late Right Hon. William Pitt from the calumnies against him, in . . . . . the Edinburgh Review for April 1810* Edinburgh, 1810.

166. Warner, Richard. *National Blessings reasons for National Gratitude: a sermon . . . . . and a character of the late Right Hon. W. Pitt* Bath, 1806.

167. In addition there is: a 26 column obituary notice of Pitt in *The Annual Register* for 1806, p. 873–887

See also Section VIII

Poetic Tributes to Pitt

168. Archilochus Jun. [pseud.] *The Volunteer Laureate: or Fall of Peter Pindar* London, 1796.

Contains an Ode to Pitt.

169. *Billy Pitt and the Union* [Dublin, 1798].
   A song.
170. Canning, George. *The Pilot who weather'd the storm.*
   A song written for the public dinner to celebrate Pitt's birthday in 1802: often reprinted it is to be most readily found in Earl Stanhope's biography of Pitt.
171. *Elijah's Mantle; being verses occasioned by the death of the Right Honourable William Pitt* [1806].
   Originally a broadsheet, also printed as a pamphlet.
172. Mason, William. *Ode to the Right Hon. William Pitt* London, 1782.
173. [Maurice, Thomas.] *Elegy on the late Right Honourable William Pitt* London, 1806.
   Reprinted as p.115–123 of Maurice's long poem *Richmond Hill* London, 1807.
174. Orme, J.B. *The Muses Tribute, a monody to the memory of the Right Hon. William Pitt . . . . . with notes* London, 1806.
175. *Regular Ode; addressed to the Right Hon. William Pitt* London, 1784.

VII. Newspapers

Newspapers in this period were single folded sheets—i.e. 4 pages—carrying a lot of advertising and often reporting parliamentary speeches at length. Owing to the printing technology of the day, they had small circulations (generally under 5,000) and obviously could not afford to maintain a high-grade editorial and reporting staff. Consequently, their editorial content was often ill-informed and inaccurate, and they are thus a guide more to what it was possible to think than to what was actually being thought.

For general surveys see:

176. Aspinall, Arthur, *Politics and the Press c.1780–1850* London, 1957.
    Less a guide than a disorderly quarry of foot-note material.
177. Werkmeister, Lucyle. *The London Daily Press, 1772–1792* Lincoln, Nebraska, 1963.
178. ———. *A Newspaper History of England 1792–1793* Lincoln, Nebraska, 1967.
    Not entirely reliable perspective.

The most important newspapers were as follows:

179. *The Courier*
    Evening paper founded 1792 and having a reformist slant till the time of Pitt's death.

180. *The Gazetteer*
London's oldest morning paper, founded 1735, taken over by *The Morning Post* in 1797; in the 1780s, under the direction of James Perry, it was the main Foxite organ—see Robert L. Haig, *The Gazetteer: 1735–1797: a study in the Eighteenth Century English Newspaper* Carbondale, 1960.
181. *The Morning Chronicle*
Pro-government morning paper till taken over by James Perry in 1789, when it became the main Foxite organ.
182. *The Morning Herald*
Pro-government.
183. *The Morning Post*
Pro-government.
184. *The Oracle*
Founded in 1789; pro-government.
185. *The Sun*
Evening paper founded in 1792; government financed.
186. *The Times*
Founded as *The Daily Universal Register* 1785, renamed *The Times* 1788; pro-government till about 1799; pro-Addington and increasingly anti-Pitt 1801–1804, still in the process of becoming the most authoritative newspaper in the country at the time of Pitt's death. An index for 1785–1789 has been published, 5 vols., Reading 1978–1983, and Samuel Palmer's quarterly indexes for 1790–1805, originally published Shepperton-on-Thames 1908–1925, have been reprinted by Kraus, 3 vols. Vaduz, 1965.
187. *The True Briton*
Founded in 1792 with government finance, amalgamated with *The Oracle* in 1805.

These are all London papers. The provincial press usually followed—indeed, stole from—the London papers with regard to national news, with the notable exception of *The Cambridge Intelligencer* under Benjamin Flower 1792–1799.

Two important weekly papers were as follows:

188. *The Anti-Jacobin; or Weekly Examiner*
Issued 1797–1798, written by George Canning and other clever young men of the ministerial clique, with occasional contributions from Pitt himself. See no. 64.
189. *Cobbett's Weekly Political Register,* from 1802 onwards: the outstanding achievement of political journalism of the period and, from 1804, virulently hostile to the Pitt system.

VIII. Biographies of Pitt

** indicates especially useful works

190. *Annals of the life of the Rt. Hon. William Pitt* Norwich [1806?].
    Based mainly on parliamentary debates.
191. Brougham, Henry Lord. *Historical Sketches of Statesmen who flourished in the Time of George III* 2 vols. London, 1839.
    Contains a 15 page critical study of Pitt, written by one of the greatest politicians of the following generation.
192. Brown, Peter Douglas. 'William Pitt "the Younger"' article in Herbert Van Thal ed. *The Prime Ministers* 2 vols. London 1974–1975.
    Negligible.
193. Butler, H. M. *Ten Great and Good Men* London, 1909.
    Pp. 30–67 deal with different aspects of Pitt's career including his eloquence, his second Ministry and his death.
194. Calman, M.A. *William Pitt; étude financière et parlementaire* Paris, 1865.
    Rather feeble, even for 1865.
195. Chanin, M. *Vie de M. Pitt* Paris, 1806.
    Critical, balanced in tone, but badly informed.
196. Chastenet, Jacques. *William Pitt* Paris, 1941.
    Bland.
197. Chatterton, E. Keeble. *England's Greatest Statesman: A*

Life of William Pitt, 1759–1806 Indianapolis, 1930.
   Pleasant scholarly biography of no special value.
198. Cleland, Henry. *Memoirs of the Right Honourable William Pitt* London, 1807.
   Extremely sketchy in parts, though interesting as a balanced contemporary view; illustrated with interesting portraits of Pitt's associates and opponents.
199. Derry, John W. *William Pitt* London, 1962.
   Brief but balanced account with interesting choice of illustrations; Derry also wrote the article on Pitt in *Encyclopedia Americana.*
200. Drummond, Mary M. 'Hon. William Pitt' article in *The House of Commons 1754–1790* edited by Lewis Namier and John Brooke, 3 vols. London, 1964 (part of *The History of Parliament* series).
   5½ columns on Pitt's earlier career—see also R. G. Thorne's contribution to the following part of the series.
201. ** Ehrman, John. *The Younger Pitt* 2 vols. so far published, London 1969 and 1983.
   Absolutely outstanding in its detail and balance: as yet, only two volumes published, covering Pitt's life up to 1796: indispensable.
202. Gifford, John, [pseud. ie, John Richards Green.] *A History of the Political Life of the Right Hon. W. Pitt* 3 vols. London, 1809.
   Three large volumes culled from newspapers and *The Annual Register:* valueless.
203. Hunt, William. 'Pitt, William' article in *Dictionary of National Biography* London, 1896.
   Balanced, political narrative of no particular value.
204. Jacob, T. Evan. *The Life of William Pitt* London, 1890.
   A political biography of no special value.
205. Jarrett, Derek. *The Younger Pitt* London, 1974.
   Lots of nice pictures but a rather bland text, without much detail.
206. Juste, Theodore. *William Pitt* [Paris, 1884.]
   Brief and bald.

207. Lamartine, Alfonse de. *Biographies and Portraits of some Celebrated People* 2 vols. London, 1866.
    Vol. 1 contains 150 pages of pleasant but negligible biography of Pitt; the author was briefly President of the French Second Republic and was one of the major poets of his time.
208. [Lepitre, Albert.] *Biographies du xix^ee Siècle* [Paris 1888].
    Includes a short and valueless life of Pitt.
209. Lewis, G.C. *Essays on the Administrations of Great Britain from 1783 to 1830* Ed. E. Head, London, 1864.
    Rather boring essays of political narrative by a minor politician who was on confidential terms with the last survivors of Pitt's heyday and whose comments often reflect the opinions of people who knew Pitt.
210. Luckwaldt, Friedrich. 'William Pitt der Jüngere' *Preussische Jahrbücher* CIX (1902) p. 185–230.
    Based on secondary sources only but occasionally gives an interesting perspective.
211. Macaulay, Thomas Babington. 'Pitt, William' article in *Encyclopædia Britannica;* various editions 1859–1911, in its final printing 'shortened and readjusted'.
    A dramatic narrative, more characteristic of its author than its subject.
212. Marriott, J. A. R. 'William Pitt' *Fortnightly Review* vol. LXXIX (1906) p. 487–503.
    A pleasant account of Pitt's career.
213. Oliver, Robert T. *Four Who Spoke Out; Burke, Fox, Sheridan, Pitt* Syracuse, New York, 1946.
    A kind of comparative study, rather journalistic despite being published by a university press, not very useful on points of fact but with some interesting insights and ideas.
214. Petrie, Sir Charles. *William Pitt* London, 1935.
    Brief and of no special value.
215. ** Reilly, Robin. *Pitt the Younger 1759–1806* London, 1978.
    The most carefully researched of the briefer biogra-

phies, it brings out the details of Pitt's personal life etc. very pleasantly: not a substitute for Ehrman but a handy introduction.
216. Robertson, C. G. 'The Younger Pitt' *Quarterly Review* CCXVI (1912) p. 307–330
   A review of a number of books, including the two following items by J. H. Rose; a judicious summing up.
217. ** Rose, John Holland. *William Pitt and National Revival* London, 1911.
218. **———. *William Pitt and the Great War* London, 1911.
   Till recently the standard biography, even now it has not been totally superseded by Ehrman; the two parts, originally published separately and some months apart, were later republished as one volume, *Life of William Pitt* London, 1923
219. ———. *A Short Life of William Pitt* London, 1925.
220. **Archibald, 5th Earl of Rosebery. *Pitt* London, 1918.
   Another very useful introduction: it is organised by themes—e.g., War, Domestic Policy, Ireland—rather than along chronological lines, and the mere fact that its author had himself been prime minister makes it worthy of attention.
221. Salomon, Felix. *William Pitt der Jüngere* vol 1 [to 1793] Leipzig, 1906 [no more published].
   The first modern-style academic study, at 588 pages almost as detailed as Ehrman but very dated as well as in German: some useful European sources are cited.
222. Smith, Goldwin. *Three English Statesmen* London, 1867.
   About half the book deals with Pitt: negligible.
(58) **Stanhope, Philip Henry, Earl. *Life of the Right Honourable William Pitt* 4 vols. London, 1862.
   One of the outstanding examples of biography in the nineteenth century, it is still useful since, unlike Rose's and Ehrman's biographies, it prints many of Pitt's letters *in extenso;* it is also worth paying attention to the balance and emphasis of Stanhope's narrative as he was much closer to Pitt in his sense of values, as a

relative and almost contemporary, than it is possible for any modern biographer to be.

223. ** Thorne, R.G. 'Hon. William Pitt' article in *The House of Commons 1790–1820* edited by R.G. Thorne, 5 vols. London, 1986 (part of *The History of Parliament* series).
A symmetrical 33½ column model of elegant compression: a small masterpiece.

224. Tomline, George Pretyman. *Memoirs of the Life of the Right Honourable William Pitt* 2 vols. London, 1821.
Of this, the 'official' biography by Pitt's former tutor, secretary, confidant and executor, the Earl of Rosebery wrote, 'There is no drearier book in all biography'. Tomline made no visible use of the manuscript material at his disposal and largely paraphrased *The Annual Register* and other published sources. The second half of Pitt's career is not covered. Rosebery, in *Bishop Tomline's Estimate of Pitt* London, 1903, discusses such minor illuminations as may be culled from this compilation and prints the previously suppressed final chapter.

225. Viel-Castel, Baron Louis de. *Essai sur les Deux Pitts* 2 vols. Paris, 1845.
Of no interest.

226. Walford, Edward. *William Pitt: A Biography* London, 1890.
Bland, and of no special value.

227. Whibley, Charles. *William Pitt* London, 1906.
Bland, and of no special value.

228. Wilson, P.W. *William Pitt, the Younger* New York, 1930.
Merely a pot-boiler.

IX. Contemporary Memoirs and Diaries Etc. Containing Important Material on Pitt
(See also Section III)

229. Abbot, Charles, Lord Colchester. *The Diary and Correspondence of Charles Abbot, Lord Colchester* edited by the 2nd Lord Colchester. 3 vols. London, 1861.
    Abbot succeeded Addington as Speaker of the House of Commons.
230. Burges, James Bland. *Selections from the correspondence of Sir James Bland Burgess, Bart* edited by James Hutton.
    Contains reminiscences of Pitt by a former junior minister, written c. 1818.
231. Douglas, Sylvester, Lord Glenbervie. *The Diaries of Sylvester Douglas (Lord Glenbervie)* edited by Francis Bickley, 2 vols. London, 1928.
    Covers period from December 1793 onwards: Douglas's diary for January–December 1793 has been published in *The Glenbervie Journals* edited by Walter Sichel, London, 1910; Douglas, a minor office holder, was rather a bore but kept one of the best diaries of the period.
232. Elliot, Gilbert, Lord Minto. *Life and Letters of Gilbert Elliot, First Earl of Minto from 1751 to 1806* edited by

[Emma Eleanor Elizabeth Elliot-Murray Kynynmound] Countess of Minto 3 vols. London, 1874.

Minto was a prominent Portland Whig, with an interesting, independent view of affairs.

233. Farington, Joseph. *The Diary of Joseph Farington* edited by Kenneth Garlick, Angus Macintyre, Kathryn Cave, 16 vols. New Haven, 1978–1984.

Farington was a fashionable topographical painter and his diary contains much gossip and contemporary comment; no index has been published as yet, but an earlier, shorter, less scholarly edition, *The Farington Diary* London, 1922–1928 has indexes.

234. Fitzroy, Augustus Henry, Duke of Grafton. *Autobiography and Political Correspondence of Augustus Henry Third Duke of Grafton K.G.* edited by Sir William R. Anson, London, 1898.

Contains important material on the 1783–1784 crisis by a close associate of Pitt's father; includes a single letter from Pitt 1783.

235. Fox, Charles James. *Memorials and Correspondence of Charles James Fox* edited by Lord John Russell, 4 vols. London, 1853–1857.

Without appearing in person, Pitt haunts vols 2–4 as the inescapable background fact determining all Fox's feverish political scheming during a period of nearly 24 years.

236. Francis, Sir Philip. *The Memoirs of Sir Philip Francis, K.C.B.* edited by J. Parkes and H. Merivale, 2 vols. London, 1867.

The appendix to volume 2 contains a brilliantly destructive character sketch of Fox, with some ferocious side swipes at Pitt, part of which has been reprinted in a somewhat unsatisfactory collection, A. D. Harvey, ed., *English Literature and the Great War with France* London, 1981.

237. Harris, James, Earl of Malmesbury. *Diaries and Correspondence of James Harris, Earl of Malmesbury* edited by the 3rd Earl of Malmesbury 4 vols. London, 1845.

Malmesbury was the leading diplomat of his day, though evidently bitterly jealous of Lord Grenville, the Foreign Secretary; a very illuminating source, and not only on the diplomatic side.

238. Leveson Gower, Granville, Earl Granville. *Private Correspondence 1781 to 1821* edited by Castalia Countess Granville, 2 vols. London, 1916.

Lord Granville Leveson was an intimate of Canning's, and the lover of the Countess of Bessborough, one of the great Whig ladies; rather a bore himself, but some of his correspondents wrote letters as good as Byron's.

239. Pratt, John Jeffreys, Earl Camden. Untitled Memorandum published in Richard Willis: 'William Pitt's Resignation in 1801: Re-examination and Document' *Bulletin of the Institute of Historcial Research* vol. XLIV (1971) p. 239–257.

An interesting source for Pitt's relations with George III, the original of the document being preserved at the Kent Archives Office, Maidstone.

240. Rogers, Samuel. *Recollections* edited by William Sharpe, London, 1859.

Records some of Lord Grenville's reminiscences of Pitt.

241. Scarlett, Peter Campbell. *A Memoir of the Right Honourable James, First Lord Abinger* London, 1877.

Contains, p. 56–58, an eye-witness account of Pitt as a parliamentary speaker.

242. Temple-Nugent-Brydges-Chandos-Grenville, Richard Plantagenet, Duke of Buckingham and Chandos. *Memoirs of the Court and Cabinets of George III* 4 vols. London, 1853–1855.

Contains important correspondence of the Grenville family, though the connecting text, which was ghost-written, is fairly worthless.

243. Windham, William. *The Diary of the Right Hon. William Windham, 1784–1810* edited by Mrs Henry Baring, London, 1866.

One of those diaries which damages rather than enhances posthumous reputations, but contains some useful material.

244. Wraxall, Sir Nathaniel. *The Historical and Posthumous Memoirs of Sir Nathaniel William Wraxall 1772–1784* edited by Henry B. Wheatley, 5 vols. London, 1884.

   Originally published as *Historical Memoirs of my Own Time* 2 vols. London, 1815 and *Posthumous Memoirs of my Own Time* 3 vols. London, 1836 these in fact cover the period up to 1789; racy, readable, quotable and completely unreliable.

245. In addition, one should consult: Dorothy Marshall. *The Rise of George Canning* London, 1938 which, though a modern scholarly biographical study, quotes very extensively from Canning's letters now preserved in Leeds Central Library and is an indispensable text with regard to Canning's relations with Pitt during the last 10 years of Pitt's life.

X. Special Topics

The notes on Sources in John Ehrman's biography (no. 201) are a wonderful quarry for references on particular topics, and are the starting place for a systematic study of any aspect of Pitt's career. The following, without intending to provide general bibliographies, indicates material specifically relating to Pitt at various stages in his career. The topics are arranged chronologically. See also Section VI. B.

Pitt's Relations with the Earl of Shelburne, 1782–1783

246. Fitzmaurice, Lord Edmond. *Life of William Earl of Shelburne* 3 vols. London, 1875–1876, revised ed. 2 vols. London, 1912.
    Old-fashioned Life and Letters: some original source material.
247. Norris, John. *Shelburne and Reform* London, 1963.
    Deals with Pitt in passing; suggestive on his relationship with Shelburne.

Pitt's Establishment in Power, and Style of Government

248. Barnes, Donald Grove. *George III and William Pitt, 1783–1806* Stanford, 1939.
    Old-fashioned constitutional history, insensitive both to the mechanics of power in Hanoverian Britain and to the peculiarities of the personalities involved.

249. Breihan John. R. 'William Pitt and the Commission on Fees, 1785–1801' *Historical Journal* XXVII (1984) p. 59–81.
   Shows how Pitt held back on implementing the reforms initiated at the beginning of his ministry.
250. Derry, J.W. *The Regency Crisis and the Whigs, 1788–1789* Cambridge, 1963.
   Despite its title, the best introduction to the Regency Crisis from Pitt's point of view.
251. Eyck, Erich. *Pitt versus Fox; Father & Son; 1735–1806* London, 1950 [original German language version Zurich, 1946].
   A group biography, rather popular in tone but providing some interesting perspectives.
252. Kelly, Paul. 'British Party Politics, 1784–1786' *Historical Journal* XVII (1974) p. 33–53.
253. ———. 'British Politics, 1783–1784: the emergence and triumph of the younger Pitt's administration' *Bulletin of the Institute of Historical Research* LIV (1981) p. 62–78.
254. ———. 'The Establishment of Pitt's Administration 1783–6' Oxford University D. Phil Dissertation, 1971.
255. ———. 'The Pitt-Temple Administration, 19–22 December 1783' *Historical Journal* XVII (1974) p. 157–161.
256. ———. 'Pitt versus Fox: The Westminster Scrutiny, 1784–5' *Studies in Burke and His Time* XIV (1972–3) p. 155–162.
257. Laprade, W.T. 'William Pitt and Westminster Elections' *American Historical Review* vol. XVIII (1913) p. 253–274.
   Deals with Pitt's campaign to unseat Fox in 1784 and 1785.
258. Rose, John Holland. 'Pitt and the Triple Alliance' *Edinburgh Review* CCXI (1910) p. 62–84.
   Discusses Pitt's foreign policy, 1788–91 including the alliance with Prussia and the Netherlands.
259. Schweitzer, David R. 'The Failure of William Pitt's Irish Trade Propositions 1785' *Parliamentary History* 3 (1984) p. 129–145.

Shows that Pitt underestimated opposition to his proposals, partly through ignoring advice from the officials in Dublin.
260. Smith, E. Anthony. 'Earl Temple's Resignation, 22 Dec. 1783' *Historical Journal* vol VI (1963) p. 91–97

Pitt's Peacetime Financial Administration

261. Audigier, Pierre Jacques. *William Pitt et la politique financière de l'Angleterre de 1782 à 1792* Paris 1929.
    French doctoral thesis.
262. Bowden, Witt. 'The Influence of the Manufacturers on some of the early Policies of William Pitt' *American Historical Review* vol XXIV (1923–1924) p. 655–674.
    On commercial relations with Ireland.
263. Cone, Carl B. 'Richard Price and Pitt's Sinking Fund of 1786' *Economic History Review* 2nd series vol. IV (1951–1952) p. 243–251.
    Attributes sinking fund to the influence of Richard Price—not the view more recently adopted by Ehrman.
264. Hoh-Cheung and Lorna A. Mui. 'William Pitt and the Enforcement of the Commutation Act, 1784–1788' *English Historical Review* vol. LXXVI (1961) p. 447–465
    On tea duties.
265. Moret y Prendergast, Segismondo. *The Financial Policy of William Pitt* London, 1888.
    Translation of a lecture by a noted Spanish statesman and political economist.
266. Sinclair, Sir John. *History of the Public Revenue of the British Empire . . . . . With a review of the financial administration of the Right Honourable William Pitt* 3rd edition 3 vols. London, 1803–1804.
    An updating of a work first published in 1785; an indefatigable bore, Sinclair was the period's leading writer on economic topics and is often surprisingly helpful.

Pitt and the French Revolution

267. Adams, Ephraim Douglas. *The Influence of Grenville on Pitt's Foreign Policy, 1787–1798* Washington, 1904.
    Short but detailed diplomatic study, useful as an introduction to its subject and the sources but weak on grasp of policy-making processes.
268. Evans, Howard V. 'William Pitt, William Miles and the French Revolution' *Bulletin of the Institute of Historical Research* vol XLIII (1970) p. 190–212.
    Deals with the outbreak of war and Pitt's later strained relations with the diplomatic agent William Augustus Miles.
269. Fitzpatrick, Walter. Introductions to *Historical Manuscripts Commission Report on the Manuscripts of J. B. Fortescue, Esq., preserved at Dropmore* [*HMC Dropmore Mss*] especially to vols. 3–7, published 1899–1910.
    Brilliant narrative and analysis.
270. Jupp, Peter. *Lord Grenville, 1759–1834* Oxford, 1985.
    Grenville, Pitt's Foreign Secretary 1791–1801, after years of neglect by historians, has finally been treated to a biography as long-winded and pedestrian as one of his own speeches; painstaking though inaccurate on minor details and ponderously balanced, it offers a useful corrective to some of the wilder interpretations of British foreign policy, but it is not easy to see the diplomat and political thinker in Professor Jupp's creakingly compartmentalised analysis of diplomacy and political thought.
271. Laprade, William Thomas. *England and French Revolution 1789–1797* Baltimore, 1909.
    Confidently written but perfectly wrong-headed doctoral dissertation arguing that Pitt and his supporters encouraged public hostility to the French Revolution in order to justify a war with France aimed at grabbing French colonies and in order to strengthen Pitt's domestic position by splitting the Foxite Whigs (see next sub-section); interesting, implausible and without hard evidence.

272. Marsh, Herbert. *The History of the Politicks of Great Britain, from the time of the Conference at Pillnitz to the Declaration of War against Great Britain* 2 vols. London, 1800.
   Still the best introduction to the relevant documents.
273. Mathiez, Albert. 'Danton, Talon, Pitt et la Mort de Louis XVI *Annales Révolutionnaires* VIII (1916) p. 367–376.
   Argues that Pitt took a strictly pragmatic, unsentimental view of the consequences to Britain of the execution of Louis XVI.
274. Stoker, John T. *William Pitt et la Révolution Française* Paris, 1935.
   French doctoral thesis by an Englishman—not very brilliant but makes extensive use of French diplomatic archives.

Accession of the Portland Whigs to Pitt's Government

275. Mitchell, L.G. *Charles James Fox and the Disintegration of the Whig Party, 1782–1794* Oxford, 1971.
   Competent but uninspiring survey.
276. O'Gorman, F. *The Whig Party and the French Revolution* London, 1967.
   Deals mainly with the Portland Whigs.
277. Rose, J. Holland. 'Burke, Windham and Pitt' *English Historical Review* vol. XXVII (1912) p. 700–716 and vol. XXVIII (1913) p. 86–105.
   Covers period 1794–1797.

Conduct of the War with France

278. Cooper, R.A. 'British Government Finance, 1793–1807. The Development of a Policy Based on War Taxes'. University of North Carolina Ph.D. Dissertation 1976.
   Microfilm order no., DDJ 77-17417.
279. ———. 'William Pitt, Taxation and the Needs of War' *Journal of British Studies* vol. XXII/1 (1982) p. 94–103.
   A summary of the main part of the preceding item: uninspiring.

280. Fortescue, J.W. *British Statesmen and the Great War 1793–1814* Oxford, 1911.
   Classic, highly prejudiced presentation of the strategic incompetence of Pitt and his colleagues.
281. O'Brien, P.K. 'Government Revenue 1793–1815: A Study in Fiscal and Financial Policy in the Wars against France' Oxford D. Phil. dissertation, 1967.
   An outstanding doctoral dissertation, providing a detailed analysis of policy in the 1790s (and after) and a valuable bibliography.
282. Mackesy, Piers. *Statesmen at War: the Strategy of Overthrow 1798–1799* London, 1974.
283. ———. *War Without Victory: the Downfall of Pitt, 1799–1802* Oxford, 1984.
   Elegantly written and exhaustively researched studies of cabinet government, decision making and the interplay of personality, against a clearly presented background of continent-wide war.
284. Manes, Alfred. 'Die Einkommensteuer in der englischen Finanz-Politik und-Literatur bis zu William Pitts Tod' *Festgaben für Wilhelm Lexis zur siebzigsten Wiederkehr seines Geburtstages* Jena, 1907 p. 100–220.
   Pp. 170–220 deal with Pitt's income tax.
285. Sherwig, John M. *Guineas and Gunpowder: British Foreign Aid in the Wars with France* Cambridge, Mass 1969.
   Well-written narrative and analysis of the policy of subsidising European allies in the struggle with France, as pursued by Pitt and his successors; Karl F. Helleiner *The Imperial Loans: A Study in Financial and Diplomatic History,* Oxford, 1965 is a much narrower and less illuminating study on the same subject.

The Legislative Union with Ireland

286. Bolton, G.C. *The Passing of the Irish Act of Union: A study in Parliamentary Politics* London, 1966.
   The archetypal OUP Oxford Historical Monograph.

287. Murphy, James McLane. 'The Pitt Administration and the Irish Roman Catholics' Fordham University Ph.D. dissertation 1968—microfilm order No. 69-02601.

The Campaign to Abolish the Slave Trade

288. Lipscomb, Patrick Cleburne. 'William Pitt and the Abolition of the Slave Trade.' University of Texas, Austin, Ph.D. dissertation 1960—microfilm order No. 60-01984.
289. ———. 'William Pitt and the Abolition Question: A Review of an Historical Controversy' *Leeds Philosophical and Literary Society Proceedings, Literary and Historical Section* XII (1967) p. 87–128.
See also Robert Isaac and Samuel Wilberforce. *The Life of William Wilberforce* 5 vols. London, 1838 already listed (no. 60); Wilberforce, one of Pitt's closest friends, was, of course, the leader of the campaign to abolish the Slave Trade.

Relations with Henry Addington after 1801

290. Harvey, A.D. *Britain in the Early Nineteenth Century* London, 1978.
Pending the completion of Ehrman's *Pitt the Younger*, provides by far the most detailed and exhaustively researched account of the final five years of Pitt's career.
291. Sack, James J. *The Grenvillites, 1801–1829: party politics and factionalism in the age of Pitt and Liverpool* Urbana, 1979.
Deals in part with Lord Grenville's attempts to mobilise Pitt against Addington.
292. Ziegler, Philip. *Addington, A Life of Henry Addington, First Viscount Sidmouth* London, 1965.
A competent biography, dealing with the Pitt-Addington relationship in the course of the narrative.

In addition:

293. Derry, John. 'Government Temperament under Pitt and Liverpool' in John Cannon ed. *The Whig Ascendancy: Colloquies on Hanoverian England* London, 1981 p. 125–145 (plus discussion p. 146–150).

    Attempts to give an overview of Tory government 1784–1827.

XI. Portraits Etc.

294. George Scharf. *A Catalogue of All Known Portraits, Busts, Engravings from Portraits &c. of William Pitt* London, 1886
    Lists 161 items 1779–1862, 84 of them posthumous.
295. Thomas Gainsborough produced 8 different versions of a portrait of Pitt in 1788.
296. John Hoppner produced 3 different versions of a portrait of Pitt in 1805–1806, of which perhaps the most important, a three-quarter length painted for Lord Mulgrave, had at least 9 contemporary copies, one of which is in the National Portrait Gallery, London.
297. Thomas Lawrence's posthumous portrait of 1808 exists in 2 different versions.
298. There is a water-colour of Pitt by James Gillray of 1789, in the National Portrait Gallery, London.
299. Anton Hickel's 'William Pitt addressing the House of Commons on the declaration of war, 1793', a group portrait of most of the M.P.'s painted 1793–1795 is in the National Portrait Gallery, London.
300. Richard Westmacott's monument to Pitt in Westminster Abbey dates from 1813.
301. Joseph Nollekens' statue in the Senate House, Cambridge, dates from 1815, though Nollekens had executed a bust of Pitt in 1806, on the basis of Pitt's death mask and Lord Mulgrave's Hoppner portrait.
302. Francis Chantrey's statue in Hanover Square, London dates from 1831.

303. Literally hundreds of contemporary caricatures featuring Pitt are listed and painstakingly described in volumes 6–8 of Mary Dorothy George's *Catalogue of Political and Personal Satires Preserved in the Department of Prints and Drawings in the British Museum* London, 1938–1947 (reprinted 1978). All 17,000 prints in the British Museum—mostly, of course, from other periods—are available in microfilm published by Chadwyck-Healey Ltd., Cambridge in 1978. Some of the prints dealing with Pitt are reproduced in two Chadwyck-Healey publications, John Brewer, ed. *The Common People and Politics 1750–1790* Cambridge, 1986 and H. T. Dickinson, ed., *Caricatures and the Constitution 1760–1832* Cambridge, 1986.

XII. Places Associated with Pitt

304. *Hayes, Kent*
     The mansion, just north of Hayes Common, where Pitt was born and brought up, has long since been demolished and the site overrun by suburbia. Chatham Avenue, Bromley approximately corresponds to the original location of the house and garden.
305. *Pembroke Hall, now Pembroke College, Cambridge*
     Pitt had the rooms over the main gate, formerly occupied by Thomas Gray, the poet, and still in existence today.
306. *Holwood, just under 4 miles south-west of Bromley, Kent*
     The small Jacobean house purchased as a country retreat by Pitt in 1785 and enlarged by John Soane burnt down in the 1820s but part of the garden laid out by Humphry Repton is still visible.
307. *Burton Pynsent, 3 miles south-west of Langport, Somerset*
     This was Pitt's father's main seat and his mother lived there as a widow until her death in 1803, Pitt being a frequent visitor; only the part built by Pitt's father survives, the rest of the house that Pitt knew having been demolished in 1805.
308. *Lincoln's Inn, London*
     When in London, in the years 1780–1782, Pitt lived in rooms on the north side of the top floor of Staircase 4, Stone Buildings, Lincoln's Inn, the part nearest High Holborn.

309. *10 Downing Street, London, SW1*
   Pitt lived here for the best part of 22 years and, after his death, it was a matter of dispute whether he had occupied the house by virtue of being First Lord of the Treasury or by virtue of being Chancellor of the Exchequer. The house is still there, of course, though much reconstructed, and heavily guarded as it is still the official residence of the prime minister. Pitt's study, overlooking the garden, is in the part of the house now occupied by the Cabinet Room.
310. *Walmer Castle, 2 miles south of Deal, Kent*
   A sixteenth-century coastal defence fortress, Walmer Castle was Pitt's official residence as Lord Warden of the Linque Ports from 1792, and he spent much time here 1801–1804; despite some subsequent additions, it remains much as he knew it. See no. 48.
311. *12 Park Place, London, SW1*
   Pitt rented this house after vacating 10 Downing Street, 1801–1802; the façade was subsequently altered.
312. *[?] 15 Johnstone Street, Bath*
   Pitt spent much of 1802 taking the waters at Bath and though according to Earl Stanhope he lived in Great Pulteney Street, the local tradition used to be that he lived around the corner at 15 Johnstone Street.
313. *14 York Place, now 120 Baker Street, London, W1*
   Pitt lived here during the parliamentary session in 1803–1804 and here awaited the collapse of Addington's ministry; now a stationers' shop with a blue plaque.
314. *Bowling Greek House, Putney Heath, London, SW15*
   Pitt leased this attractive villa—illustrated in J. Holland Rose's *William Pitt and the Great War*—from 1804 and died there. The house was demolished in the early 1930s and the site is now occupied by Bowling Green Close, consisting of ugly and expensive houses mostly bearing names with a Pitt/Chatham/Holwood theme.

Index of Authors and Titles

references are to item numbers

Abbot, Charles, Lord Colchester, 229
Adam, Ephraim Douglas, 267
Adams, William, 65
Addington (Ziegler), 292
Addington, Henry, Life and Correspondence of (Pellew), 55
American Historical Review, 257, 262
Annales Révolutionnaires, 273
Annual Register, 63, 167
Anti-Jacobin; or Weekly Examiner, 64, 188
Ashbourne, Edward 1st Lord, 36
Aspinall, Arthur, 37, 38, 176
Auckland, Lord, Journal and Correspondence of (Hogge), 40
Audigier, Pierre Jacques, 261

Barnes, Donald Grove, 248
Beddoes, Thomas, 134
Bentley, Thomas Richard, 143, 144
Biographies and Portraits of some Celebrated People (Lamartine), 207
Biographies du xixe siècle (Lepitre), 208
Bisset, Robert, 145
Black, Jeremy, 54
Bolton, G. C., 286
Bowden, Witt, 262
Breihan, John R., 249

Bridge J., 68
Britain in the Early Nineteenth Century (Harvey) 290
British Statesmen and the Great War 1793–1814 (Fortescue), 280
Brougham, Henry, 191
Brown, Peter Douglas, 192
Buckingham and Chandos, Duke of: see Temple-Nugent-Brydges-Chandos-Grenville
Bulletin of the Institute of Historical Research, 239, 253, 268
Burges, James Bland, 230
Butler, H. M., 193

Calman, M. A., 194
Camden, Earl: see Pratt, John Jeffreys
Canning, George, 170
Canning, George, The Rise of (Marshall), 245
Castlereagh, Viscount, Memoir and Correspondence of (Londonderry), 41
Chanin, M., 195
Chastenet, Jacques, 196
Chatterton, E. Keeble, 197
Cleland, Henry, 198
Cobbett, William, 61
Cone, Carl B., 263
Cooper, R. A., 278, 279
Coupland, R., 62
Courtenay, Thomas Peregnne, 146

Debrett, J., 61

Derry, John Wesley, 199, 250, 293
Dictionary of National Biography, 203
Douglas, Sylvester, Lord Glenbervie, 231
Drennan, William, 130, 131
Drummond, Mary M., 200
Durham University Journal, 54

Economic History Review, 263
Edinburgh Review, 258
Effingham, Richard Howard 4th Earl of, 114
Ehrman, John, 201
Eldon, Lord Chancellor, The Public and Private Life of (Twiss), 59
Elliot, Gilbert, Lord Minto, 232
Encyclopedia Americana, 199
Encyclopædia Britannica, 211
England and the French Revolution, 1789–1797 (Laprade), 271
English Historical Review, 264, 277
Essays on the Administrations of Great Britain from 1783 to 1830 (Lewis), 209
Evans, Howard V., 268
Eyck, Erich, 251

Farington, Joseph, 233
Fitzmaurice, Lord Edmond, 246
Fitzpatrick, Walter, 269
Fitzroy, Augustus Henry, Duke of Grafton, 234
Fortescue, J. W., 280
Fortnightly Review, 212
Fox, Charles James, 235
Francis, Sir Philip, 236

Gam, David, 137
Gazetteer: 1735–1797 (Haig), 180
George, Prince of Wales, 1770–1812, The Correspondence of (Aspinall), 38
George III, The Later Correspondence of (Aspinall), 37
George III and William Pitt (Barnes), 248
Gifford, John, 202

Glenbervie, Lord: *see* Douglas, Sylvester
Grafton, Duke of: see Fitzroy, Augustus Henry
Grenville, Influence of, on Pitt's Foreign Policy (Adams), 267
Grenville, Lord, 1759–1834 (Jupp), 270
Grenvillites, 1801–1829 (Sack), 291
Guineas and Gunpowder (Sherwig), 285

Haig, Robert L., 180
Hamiilton, Lord Archibald, 154
Hansard, T. C., 61
Harcourt, L. V., 39
Harris, James, Earl of Malmesbury, 237
Harvey, A. D., 236, 290
Hathaway, W. S., 62
Helleiner, Karl F., 286
Historical Journal, 249, 252, 255, 260
Historical Sketches of Statesmen who flourished in the Time of George III (Brougham), 191
History of the Politicks of Great Britain (Marsh), 272
History of the Public Revenue of the British Empire (Sinclair), 266
Hogge, George, 40
Hoh-Cheung, 264
Horne Tooke, John, 139
House of Commons 1754–1790 (Namier and Brooke), 200
House of Commons 1790–1820 (Thorne), 223
Howlett, John, 128
Hunt, William, 203

Imperial Loans (Helleiner), 285
Irish Act of Union, The Passing of (Bolton), 286

Jacob, T. Evan, 204
Jarrett, Derek, 205
Jones, Stephen, 158, 159
Journal of British Studies, 279

Index

Jupp, Peter, 270
Juste, Theodore, 206

Kelly, Paul, 252–256

Lamartine, Alfonse de, 207
Laprade, William Thomas, 257, 271
Laurence, French, 99
Leeds Philosophical and Literary Society, Proceedings, 289
Lepitre, Albert, 208
Leveson Gower, Lord Granville, 238
Lewis, G. C., 209
Lipscomb, Patrick Cleburne, 288, 289
Londonderry, Charles 3rd Marquis of, 41
Luckwaldt, Friedrich, 210

Macaulay, Thomas Babington, 211
Mackesy, Piers, 282, 283
Mahon, Lord: *see* Stanhope, Philip Henry, 5th Earl
Malmesbury, Earl of: *see* Harris, James
Manes, Alfred, 284
Marriott, J. A. R., 212
Marsh, Herbert, 272
Marshall, Dorothy, 245
Mason, William, 172
Mathiez, Albert, 273
Maurice, Thomas, 173
Meadley, G. W., 80
Melville, Lewis, 42
Mitchell, L. G., 275
Moret y Prendergast, Segismondo, 265
Morgan, William, 118–121 (and cf. 124–7)
Mui Lorna A., 264
Murphy, James McLane, 287

Norris, John, 247

O'Brien, P. K., 281
O'Gorman, F., 276
Oliver, Robert T., 213
Orme, J. B., 174

Parliamentary Debates from the Year 1803 to the Present Time (Cobbett and Hansard), 61
Parliamentary History, 259
Parliamentary History of England, from the Earliest Period to the Year 1803 (Cobbett), 61
Parliamentary Register (Debrett), 61
Pasquin, Anthony, 141
Pellew, George, 55
Petrie, Sir Charles, 214
Phipps, Edmund, 56
Pitt versus Fox: Father & Son: 1735–1806 (Eyck), 251
Pindar, Peter, 87–92
Pitt, William, A Catalogue of All Known Portraits of (Scharf), 294
Pitt, Right Hon. William, and Charles Duke of Rutland, Lord Lieutenant of Ireland, 1781–1787, Correspondence Between, 46
Pitt and Napoleon: Essays and Letters (Rose), 43
Pitt, William, and National Revival (Rose), 217
Pitt, William, and the Great War (Rose), 218
Pitt and Wilberforce (Rosebery), 44
Pitt, William, et la Révolution Française (Stoker), 274
Pitt, William, The Financial Policy of (Moret y Prendergast), 265
Pitt, the Right Honourable William, The Speeches of (Hathaway), 62
Pitt, William, the Younger, the War Speeches of (Coupland), 62
Pitt's Foreign Policy, The Influence of Grenville on (Adam) (*see also* 36, 58, 190–228), 267
Pitt, William, Earl of Chatham, Correspondence of, 50
Plummer, T., 110
Politics and the Press c1780–1850 (Aspinall), 176
Pratt, John Jeffreys, 2nd Earl Camden, 239
Prime Ministers (Van Thal), 192
Pringle, John Henry, 50

Quarterly Review, 216

Regency Crisis and the Whigs, 1788–1789 (Derry), 250
Reilly, Robin, 215
Richardson, Joseph, 99
Robertson, C. G., 216
Rogers, Samuel, 240
Rolliad, Criticisms of (Richardson, Tickell, Laurence), 99
Rose, George, 162
Rose, George, Diaries and Correspondence of, 39
Rose, John Holland, 43, 57, 217–219, 258, 277
Rosebery, Archibald Primrose, 5th Earl of, 44, 45, 220, 224

Sack, James J., 291
Salomon, Felix, 221
Scarlett, P. C., 241
Scharf, George, 294
Schweitzer, David R., 259
Sharp, James, 163
Shelburne and Reform (Norris), 247
Shelburne, Life of William Earl of (Fitzmaurice), 246
Sherwig, John M., 285
Sinclair, John, 266
Smith, E. Anthony, 260
Smith, Goldwin, 222
Stanhope, Charles, 3rd Earl, 123
Stanhope,, Philip Henry, 5th Earl, 46–49, 58
Statesmen at War: the Strategy & Overthrow 1798–1799 (Mackesy), 282
Statesmen who flourished in the Time of George III, Historical Sketches of (Brougham), 191
Stoker, John T., 274
Studies in Burke and his Time, 256

Taylor, William Stanhope, 50
Temple-Nugent-Brydges-Chandos-Grenville, Richard Plantagenet, 2nd Duke of Buckingham and Chandos, 242

Ten Great and Good Men (Butler), 193
Thorne, R. G., 223
Tickell, Richard, 99
Tomline, George Pretyman, 164, 224
Twiss, Horace, 59

Vansittart, Nicholas, 125
Van Thal, Herbert, 192
Vie-Castel, Baron Louis de, 225

Wakefield, Daniel, 126, 127
Walford, Edward, 226
Walmer Castle, Notes and Extracts of Letters referring to Mr. Pitt and (Stanhope), 48
War Without Victory: the Downfall of Pitt, 1799–1802 (Mackesy), 283
Ward, Robert, 152
Ward, Robert Plumer, Memoirs of the Political and Literary Life of (Phipps), 56
Warner, Richard, 166
Werkmeister, Lucyle, 177, 178
Whibley, Charles, 227
Whig Ascendancy, 293
Whig Party and the French Revolution (O'Gorman), 276
Wilberforce, A. M., 51
Wilberforce, Robert Isaac and Samuel (and cf. 289) 52, 60
Wilberforce, William, Correspondence of, 52
Wilberforce, William, Life of, 60
Wilberforce, William, Private Papers of, 51
Williams John: *see* Pasquin, Anthony
Willis, Richard, 239
Wilson, P. W., 228
Windham Papers (Melville), 42
Windham, William, 243
Wolcot, John: *see* Pindar, Peter
Wraxall, Nathaniel, 244
Wyvill, Christopher, 53

Ziegler, Philip, 292

Index of Correspondents and Topics

references are to item numbers

Aberdeen, George Hamilton Gordon, 4th Earl of (1784–1860), 9(q)
Addington, Henry, later 1st Viscount Sidmouth (1757–1844) (see also 292), 5(a) 55
Addington, Pitt's Relations with, 5(a) 47, 55, 143–155, 291–293
Amherst, Jeffrey Amherst, 1st Baron (1717–1797), 13(a)
Auckland, William Eden, 1st Baron (1744–1814), 7, 9(c) 9(s) 28(b) 40, 45

Bathurst, Henry Bathurst, 3rd Earl (1762–1834), 31
Bridport, Alexander Hood, 1st Viscount (1727–1814), 9(e)
Buccleuch, Henry Scott, 3rd Duke of (1746–1812), 4(a)
Burke, Edmund (1729–1797), 19
Burke, Richard (1758–1794), 16, 19

Camden, John Jeffreys Pratt, 2nd Earl (1759–1840) (see also 239), 13(b)
Canning, George (1770–1827), 8
Carlisle, Frederick Howard, 5th Earl of (1748–1825), 32
Castlereagh, Robert Stewart, styled Viscount (1769–1822), 41
Chatham, Hester Pitt, Countess of (d. 1803), 12(a), 26, 50, 54
Chatham, John Pitt, 2nd Earl of (1756–1835), 26

Chatham, William Pitt, 1st Earl of (1708–1778), 12(a), 26, 50

Dorset, John Frederick Sackville, 3rd Duke of (1745–1799), 13(c)
Douglas, John (1721–1807), 9(u)
Dundas, Henry, later 1st Viscount Melville (1742–1811), 4(c), 9(m), 14(b), 26, 47

Eldon, John Scott, 1st Baron (1751–1838), 11, 47, 59

Farquhar, Sir Walter (1738–1819), 49
Financial Policies, Pitt's, 12, 113–127, 261–266
Fitzwilliam, William Wentworth Fitzwilliam, 2nd Earl (1748–1833), 16
Fox, Pitt's Relations with: *see* Opposition to Pitt
France, Pitt and the war with, 62, 107–112, 268–274, 278–285
Fuller, Stephen (fl. 1785–1789), 28(b)

George III (1738–1820), 25, 37
George, Prince of Wales, later George IV (1762–1830), 25, 38
Grafton, Augustus Henry Fitzroy, 3rd Duke of (1735–1811), 234
Grant, Sir William (1752–1832), 28(b)
Grenville, Thomas (1755–1846), 9(o)
Grenville, William Wyndham Grenville, 1st Baron (1759–1834) (see also 242), 9(t), 33

Hammond, George (1763–1853), 10

Hardwicke, Philip Yorke, 3rd Earl of (1757–1834), 9(f)
Harrowby, Dudley Ryder, 2nd Baron (1762–1847), 21
Hobart, Robert Hobart, styled Lord (1760–1816), 9(l)
Hope, Alexander (1769–1837), 4(b)
Huskisson, William (1770–1830), 9(k)

Irish Policy, Pitt's, 15(a), 41, 46, 129–131, 259, 262, 286, 287

Jackson, George (1725–1822), 9(b)

Kenyon, Lloyd Kenyon, 1st Baron (1732–1802), 23, 34

Leeds, Francis Osborne, 5th Duke of (1751–1799), 9(v)
Leveson Gower, Lord Granville (1773–1846), 12(b)
Liverpool, Charles Jenkinson, 1st Earl of (1727–1808), 9(i), 28(b)
Liverpool, Robert Banks Jenkinson, 2nd Earl of (1770–1828), 9(j), 10
Lonsdale, James Lowther, 1st Earl of (1736–1802), 3, 35
Lowther, William Lowther, 2nd Viscount (1757–1844), 3, 35

Mahon, Philip Henry Stanhope, styled Viscount (1781–1855), 13(d)
Middleton, Sir Charles, later 1st Baron Barham (1726–1813), 18
Muncaster, John Pennington, 1st Baron (1741–1813), 14(a)

Opposition by Pitt (1803–1804), 143–155, 291–293
Opposition to Pitt, 250–257, 271, 276, 277, 291–293
Orde, Thomas, later 1st Baron Bolton (1746–1807), 15(a)

Parliamentary Reform, Pitt and, 15(b), 53, 106
Pembroke, George Augustus Herbert, 11th Earl of (1759–1827), 22
Portland, William Henry Cavendish Bentinck, 3rd Duke of (1738–1809), 17
Portland Whigs, Pitt and the, 9(h), 17, 42, 275–277
Puisaye, *Comte* Joseph de (1755–1827), 9(a)

Richmond, Charles Lennox, 3rd Duke of (1735–1806), 31
Rose, George (1744–1818), 9(p), 26, 39
Rutland, Charles Manners, 4th Duke of (1754–1787), 15(a), 46

Scott, Sir William (1745–1836), 59
Simcoe, John Graves (1752–1806), 5(b)
Slave Trade, Pitt and the Abolition of the, 44, 51, 52, 60, 288, 289
Spencer, George John Spencer, 2nd Earl (1758–1834), 9(w)
Stafford, Granville Leveson Gower, 1st Marquis of (1721–1803), 9(p), 12(b), 20, 29
Stafford, George Granville Leveson Gower, 2nd Marquis of (1758–1833), 9(p), 20
Stanhope, Charles Stanhope, 3rd Earl (1753–1816), 49
Sydney, Thomas Townshend, 1st Viscount (1733–1800), 26

Tomline, George Pretyman (1750–1827), 1, 6

Ward, Robert (1765–1846), 56
Wellesley, Richard Colley Wellesley, 1st Marquis (1760–1842), 9(g), 26
Whigs: *see* Opposition to Pitt and Portland Whigs
Wilberforce, William (1759–1833), 28(b), 44, 51, 52, 60
Willis, Thomas (1754–1827), 9(n)
Windham, William (1750–1810) (see also 243), 9(h), 42
Wyvill, Christopher (1740–1822), 15(b), 53

Yorke, Charles Philip (1764–1834), 9(r)
Young, Arthur (1741–1820), 9(d)